Routledge Revivals

Justice and Liberty

First published in 1908, this book takes the form of a discussion between Henry Martin- a professor, Charles Stuart- a banker, and Sir John Harington- a gentleman of leisure, on politics and civilisation. The speakers discuss many topics ranging from forms of society (such as oligarchy or democracy), to the institution of marriage, to the necessity of government.

Justice and Liberty

A Political Dialogue

G. Lowes Dickinson

Routledge
Taylor & Francis Group

First published in 1908
by George Allen & Unwin LTD

This edition first published in 2016 by Routledge
2 Park Square, Milton Park, Abingdon, Oxon, OX14 4RN
and by Routledge
711 Third Avenue, New York, NY 10017

Routledge is an imprint of the Taylor & Francis Group, an informa business

Publisher's Note
The publisher has gone to great lengths to ensure the quality of this reprint but points out that some imperfections in the original copies may be apparent.

Disclaimer
The publisher has made every effort to trace copyright holders and welcomes correspondence from those they have been unable to contact.

ISBN 13: 978-1-138-95783-1 (hbk)
ISBN 13: 978-1-315-66149-0 (ebk)

JUSTICE AND LIBERTY

A POLITICAL DIALOGUE

BY

G. LOWES DICKINSON

"ES ERBEN SICH GESETZ' UND RECHTE
WIE EINE EW'GE KRANKHEIT FORT"
GOETHE

London

GEORGE ALLEN & UNWIN LTD

FIRST PUBLISHED IN 1908
REPRINTED IN 1919 AND 1943

PRINTED IN GREAT BRITAIN BY
UNWIN BROTHERS LTD., WOKING

TABLE OF CONTENTS

CONTENTS

THE SPEAKERS ARE:

HENRY MARTIN, a professor.

CHARLES STUART, a banker.

SIR JOHN HARINGTON, a gentleman of leisure.

JUSTICE AND LIBERTY

A POLITICAL DIALOGUE

Stuart. In the same place? I knew we should find you here. And always studying? **§ 1. Introduction**

Martin. Dreaming, I fear you would call it. The place invites to it. I love the sound and sight of the running water, the great green slopes fragrant with pines, and the granite cliffs shining against the sky. But to-day I am saying farewell to them. I return home to-morrow.

Harington. To-morrow! Why?

Martin. The day after is the polling-day in my constituency.

Harington. And you are really going back to vote?

Martin. Certainly. Why not?

Stuart. Don't you know he is a great politician? At the time of the Boer war I had to engage in a free fight to protect him against a hostile meeting. And it was the more provoking because, of course, I was on the other side.

Martin. Stuart has the greatest contempt for my political opinions.

JUSTICE AND LIBERTY

Introduction *Stuart.* I haven't the least objection to your opinions, so long as you don't try to bring them to bear on practice. My quarrel with you is not that you have speculative views, but that you want to apply them.

Martin. My misfortune is that I can never, with the best will in the world, dissociate practice from speculation. Really, I have tried very hard. When I was a young man, deep in philosophy, I was tormented by the obstinate persistence of the concrete world, in apparent independence of my thinking. At last I resolved to plunge into it and see what it was really made of. I became an engineer, or endeavoured to. But it was no use. The workshop led me to mechanics, and mechanics to physics, and physics back to metaphysics. The real world, as they call it, I found was nothing but a web spun out of the stuff of thought. As it stood, and as it appeared, it had for me no interest. Its interest was that it was soul embodied. And so it has been all through my life. The practical, wherever I have tried to penetrate it, in order to abide in it, has let me down and through into the speculative again.

Stuart. That means, I suppose, what I have always thought, that you were meant to be a metaphysician.

Martin. Alas, no! For the speculative, as fast, tosses me back to the practical. I am like those unhappy souls who can find no acceptance either in heaven or in hell. If I begin with Hegel I end in the stock-exchange; if I begin with the stock-exchange I end in Hegel.

A POLITICAL DIALOGUE

Stuart. And if you begin, as we did the other day, with the reform of the income-tax, you end with a discussion of the principles of Plato's " Republic." **Introduction**

Martin. It was Harington who brought us there. But the connexion is obvious enough.

Stuart. I am afraid it still escapes me.

Martin. There is about you, as about most men I have met who are engaged in business, a calm belief in the finality of the order of things in which you work which I view with as much astonishment as you do my predilection for the untried and unknown. Though you know, I suppose, in a general way, that the history of Man has been nothing but a process of transformation; and that the gulf in ideals and in achievement between an ancient Briton and a modern Englishman is as great, at least, as that between a modern Englishman and the kind of man a Utopian imagines, yet you dismiss without further ado as impracticable dreams all those visions of the future which to me are the only things much worth considering.

Stuart. I dismiss them, not because they point to an order different from that under which we live,—no doubt some different order, for better or for worse, will come about—but because I judge the proposals laid before me to be impracticable.

Martin. Yes; but why is it that you do so dogmatically judge them to be impracticable? While I find it so difficult to decide whether they are so, or no.

Introduction *Stuart.* I suppose, if I may say so without offence, because my line of life has brought me more closely into touch with realities than yours has you.

Martin. That sounds a reasonable explanation and I have often tried to accept it. I should be so glad, if I could, to get away from all these questions, on the ground of incompetence. But always, when I talk to men of business, with what I believe to be an open mind, I find myself profoundly dissatisfied. For though these men know much more than I do about affairs, and are, in many cases, at least as competent to analyse and understand what they know, yet always they have at the bottom of their minds certain fixed axioms about what is equitable or otherwise desirable, which they have never examined, which I am unable to accept, but on which, at bottom, their whole argument proceeds.

Stuart. What sort of axioms do you mean?

Martin. Well—to take the most important and the most common—that property and the family are sacred and ultimate facts, meaning by property and the family the particular arrangements we now have in those fundamental matters. So that, if any proposed change involves a radical reconstruction of those institutions, they do not really consider it even while they seem to be arguing about it, but have already rejected it before the discussion begins. And I cannot help thinking that even some of the Economists approach their subject in the same way, and with all their learning and good faith are often, without suspecting it, really rather advocates than men of science. **Introduction**

Stuart. Whether that were so or no would make no difference, if their arguments are conclusive. I do not pretend myself to be free from prejudices—I don't believe any one ever was or will be—but my objections to any far-reaching scheme of reform of which I have ever heard, though they may be confirmed by my prejudices, do not depend upon them. They depend upon hard reasoning.

Martin. Yes; but how hard? That is my other trouble. The difficulty about all discussion of these subjects is that at bottom you come back to supposed truths about human nature. Now the people I talk to nearly always assume that human nature is a fixed quantity which they have more or less accurately measured. But to me it is a Being in perpetual transformation. What it was a thousand years ago, it is not now, and will not be a thousand years hence. What it is in Asia or in Africa, it is not in Europe. It is a growing creature, and we know almost nothing about the laws of its growth. To fix it, then, at a certain point, to say "so it is and so it must be; and therefore only such and such a form of society is possible," is, from my point of view, preposterous. And that is why I go away dissatisfied and unconvinced from the acutest argument and the subtlest analysis, feeling

Introduction that it is all founded on assumptions that I cannot accept.

Stuart. No reasonable man imagines that there may not be changes in human nature whereby things may become possible that are not possible now. Only, we say, first change your human nature before you begin meddling with institutions.

Martin. That again sounds so reasonable, yet really, in practice, is so obstructive. For if it be true that institutions depend on human nature, it is also true that human nature depends on them, and on our ideas about them. And if you treat institutions as something sacrosanct, if you rule out all criticism of them, and all experimenting with them, you are hindering precisely the change in human nature which you say you want, by suppressing that insurrection of the spirit which alone can bring it about. It is not enough to urge the rich to be generous and chivalrous, or the poor to be patient and thrifty; such appeals leave men cold. What really stirs them is a demonstration that the order under which they live is neither reasonable nor just. They may then come to find it so intolerable that they can no longer rest in it. And then, and then only, you have the condition of your change in human nature.

Stuart. Well, there are socialists enough attempting that demonstration.

Martin. Yes; but their way of putting the case has

somehow not been successful with exactly the men who most need conversion, the able men who actually direct and control the business world.

Stuart. I suggest that the reason for that is precisely that these *are* able men.

Martin. I think not; I think the reason is that they are men of very little education, and of no imagination, outside the region of business. They do not really see the facts to which socialists call attention, because they do not really feel them. They refute, or rather they ignore, without having understood; and they have not understood because they have not appreciated. Their good faith I shall not deny; what I dispute is their competence. They have never experienced that upheaval of the soul which has made the socialist a socialist by showing him everything in a new light, both the facts of the present and the possibilities of the future. They are, I should be inclined to admit, more competent than most socialists, insomuch that I can hardly imagine any successful revolution taking place without their willing and active co-operation. But their ability, for the purposes in which I am interested, is of no use, until they have undergone some process equivalent to conversion. After conversion, it is true, they might still be against almost everything that socialists have ever proposed, though I do not think it likely that they would be. But even so, their opposition would be of a quite different kind from what it is

Introduction now. It would be that of men who want to help reform, not to hinder it. "If such and such a thing is not practicable," they would say, "then we must try so and so." Whereas now their attitude most commonly is, "we must make out that everything is impracticable, in order that nothing may be done."

Stuart. Well, if you come to that, why should anything be done of the drastic and revolutionary kind? I'm not an optimist; I think there's a great deal of evil in the world, some of which is preventible. But neither am I a pessimist. Things are tolerable as they are; society as we know it is a machine that at any rate does somehow work. Whereas, if you once begin to pull it to pieces, with a view to improving it, you may never be able to put it together again.

Martin. Do you think you would take that view, if, having all your present experience and ability, you were one of the poor, instead of one of the well-to-do?

Stuart. I think I ought to; but perhaps I should not, because I should be blinded by indignation or hope.

Martin. And are you not blinded now, if not by hope, by fear? Are we not all of us so blinded in our class,—unless, indeed, we have been converted?

Stuart. Possibly; but it is no use to exchange one bias for another.

Martin. But we may endeavour to correct the one by taking account of the other. The well-to-do, at any rate, would do well to look at society from the stand- point of the poor. Introduction

Stuart. That, it seems to me, is just what they are all doing.

Martin. Not all; and especially not those who most ought to, the business men who, for good or for evil, are responsible more than any one else for the continuance of our social order.

Stuart. It is they who need conversion?

Martin. Yes.

Stuart. Well, I am one of them, and I am here at your mercy. Convert me if you can!

Martin. Alas! I am not a prophet, nor an economist, nor even a socialist, but at best a perplexed inquirer socialistically inclined. Besides, I have first to convert Harington.

Stuart. What! do the doctors disagree?

Martin. Yes; but they agree in disagreeing with you. Harington and I both condemn our present social order, though we differ as to what we would wish to substitute.

Stuart. What is the point of difference?

Martin. Briefly, he is an aristocrat, and I am a democrat.

Stuart. Well, I'm something of an aristocrat myself, so probably I should agree with him.

Harington. That isn't likely, for I am quite as much an idealist as Martin.

Introduction *Stuart.* I suppose you are, in your haughty, remote way. But you don't obtrude your idealism as he does, for you never seem to imagine it to be practicable.

Harington. In this bad age I think nothing good practicable.

Martin. You see how difficult my position is between you both. I have to convince you of the value of ideals in general, and Harington of the preferability of my ideal to his.

Stuart. Well, if you like to spend your last day in that forlorn attempt, I have no objection.

Martin. In what way better could I spend it? If only you don't mind listening.

Stuart. Not in the least! I have a pipe.

Martin. Smoke, then, and listen, and interrupt when you feel inclined, which I hope will be often, for I mean to provoke you.

Stuart. Do, as much as you can. I have the best of tempers.

Martin. What I have to do then, so far as Harington is concerned, is to elicit the principles of his ideal, and of mine, and to compare them; and so far as you are concerned, to compare both with our existing society, and so make it clear to you that we need ideals, and definite ones, both to judge it and to improve it.

Stuart. Very good.

A POLITICAL DIALOGUE

§ 2. Forms of Society
(1) Oligarchy

Martin. I will begin, then, with a point on which both Harington and I are agreed, that by Aristocracy and Democracy we mean not forms of government, but forms of society. They are distinguishable, I mean, by the end which the community sets before itself, not merely by the number of persons in whom it vests political power.

Harington. Certainly.

Martin. And the distinction, would you agree, will be something of this kind:—Aristocracy aims at the good of a class; and Democracy at the good of the Whole?

Harington. You can hardly expect me to concede that! Aristocracy, as I conceive it, certainly aims at the good of the Whole.

Martin. Then you dissociate yourself, at the outset, from a certain modern school, who maintain that the only Good is Power; I ought to apologise to them for using the word Good, for they say there is no such thing; but though they repudiate the word, they seem to intend what it means, for they say that Power is the only thing a noble man will care to pursue; and they praise those who pursue it and despise those who do not.

Harington. Meaning by Power domination over other men?

Martin. Yes. And this domination, they hold, is in itself an end; whereas justice and kindness and

(1) Oligarchy humanity, and other such qualities, are false ideals, entertained only by the weak and the degenerate. So that, in their view, an aristocratic community would be one in which the mass of men were subject to the few, and these few exercised their power not for the Good of the subjects—for that they hold to be a base ideal—but for the sake of its life-enhancing effect upon themselves.

Harington. You are thinking, I suppose, of Nietzsche and those who profess to be his disciples. But surely it is hardly worth while to take account of them? Nietzsche himself, no doubt, was a man of genius. But owing, as I think, to his lonely and unnatural life, and in part, perhaps, to the disease of which he died, he had lost all sense of proportion. And his followers, who echo his extravagance without the excuse of his genius, seem to me very insincere and foolish people! I have, I confess, very little patience with men who, living an ordinary middle-class life, and possessing, themselves, and expecting others to possess all the characteristics of the class which they affect to despise, yet imagine they would be at home in a society in which there should be no rule but the law of the strong, and in which merely to exist, I do not say to dominate, would demand qualities, call them virtues or vices, which they are the last people likely to be able to show. A man who had the right to such opinions as these men profess would surely, in our society, become a great criminal, an active revolutionary, or anarchist; he would not compose, over his sausage and his beer, phrases to frighten children. **(1) Oligarchy**

Martin. I do not know what these gentlemen might say in their defence, if they were here. You, it seems, will not champion them, as I had half hoped; and I cannot. But putting aside these philosophers, who profess but do not practise the doctrine of Power, there have always been men in society who practise without professing it. Nietzsche's strong man is not a mere ideal; he's a fact. A Greek tyrant, or a mediæval baron, or a Renaissance prince, more often than not, was such a man. And in our own time, if report is to be believed, we find the type in the great financiers. Some of these, it would almost seem, are creditable modern representatives of Periander, or of Front-de-Boeuf, or of Cæsar Borgia. For it is Power, not wealth or comfort, at which they aim; and in pursuit of that aim they trample under foot all law and all morality. As the ancient tyrant or the mediæval baron robbed, so do they; only, where he stole lands and castles and material goods, they steal the symbols of these things, securities and cash. As the tyrant and the baron tortured and murdered, so do they; only where he with his own hands used the rack and the knife, saw the blood flow and heard the victim scream, they perhaps never see or learn the consequences of their operations, except when they read in the papers, or hear in conver-

(1) Oligarchy sation as they return from church, that this man is in the bankruptcy court, that in the lunatic asylum, while another has committed suicide leaving his wife and children destitute. But such effects, it must be presumed, according to the theory we are discussing, are delightful to them rather than otherwise; for they enhance their sense of life. Power being their ideal, they are most conscious of having achieved it when the resistance over which they have triumphed has been most vigorous; and what provokes resistance more determined than the prospect of spoliation, ruin and death? The more, therefore, the victims suffer the more "Overman" rejoices; for the more conscious he is of being strong; and in that sense of strength lies his whole satisfaction in life.

Stuart. That may be a description of Nietzsche's "Overman;" but it is an absurd caricature even of the American financier.

Martin. I will admit, if you like, that it is a caricature of both; but the fact that we cannot think it to be anything else is itself a criticism of the ideal of Power. We feel, in fact, and I think everyone would feel, that that ideal, purely, simply, and in abstraction from all others, never could be entertained by any sane man; and that the men who have entertained it—possibly there have been such—must be set aside as abnormal. Nevertheless, it is true, I believe, that the enjoyment of Power, not absolutely and at all costs, but subject to certain considerations of humanity and justice, or **(1) Oligarchy** at least of prudence, has been a main motive of all governing classes; and its maintenance, rather than the Good of the whole, the object of their polity. In the case of the typical tyrant this is obvious enough; but if he, as I have suggested, is not to be regarded as a normal type, we may find examples enough elsewhere. In every slave-owning community, for example—and in the history of the world most communities have owned slaves—the main purpose of all institutions is to preserve the supremacy of the masters; that they shall have power comes first—it is the fundamental axiom—and how they shall use it, with what measure of equity or benevolence, comes second. The same is true wherever the white race comes in contact with coloured peoples; that the white shall have power, and sole power, is the dominant consideration. Or, to take milder examples, the first object, one may fairly say, of the English aristocracy, in their great days, was to maintain and perpetuate their power; and the same purpose, it might be urged, without much exaggeration, animates the rich class that really governs our own society. History, indeed, as I read it, is an almost unbroken record of government by classes or individuals in their own interest, though I do not pretend that their government may not often and at many points have been also in the interests of the community. So far, then, they have really represented

(1) **Oligarchy** that ideal of Power attributed by Nietzsche to the "Overman." And that is why I introduced his conception at the beginning; for I thought perhaps you would be content to call such governments aristocratic, and that we might find in them illustrations of what you mean by the aristocratic principle.

Harington. If I am to defend my principle, I must defend it in its purest and most ideal form. I do not admit, as I said, that the power of the governing class is the true end of aristocracy. And all these examples you have been giving, I regard, in Aristotle's phrase, as perversions of the ideal. I would rather call them Oligarchies than Aristocracies; though properly, if the word had not received another meaning, they should be named Dynasties.

Martin. Well, no matter for the name; the important point is the definition. We have here a kind of polity whose first principle is the maintenance of the power of the governing class; and this we will call, if you like, Oligarchy. And now, how do you distinguish from this your own ideal, which you call Aristocracy?

(2) **Aristocracy** *Harington.* The principle of Aristocracy, as I understand it, is not the Power of the governing class, but the Good of the Whole.

Martin. That will serve to distinguish it from Oligarchy, but not from Democracy; for Democracy will make the same claim.

Harington. From Democracy it is distinguished by its recognition of superiority and inferiority. **(2) Aristocracy**

Martin. In its institutions, do you mean?

Harington. Yes; Aristocracy is a polity of classes. It has a governing class, a fighting class (if necessary), professional classes, labouring classes, and so on.

Martin. So far it resembles our own society.

Harington. Yes; but there are two great distinctions. Our classes, first, are not fixed and definite; men may and do pass from one to another. And, secondly, they do not correspond to faculty; for there are many men in every occupation who would really be better fitted for something else.

Martin. The classes, then, of an aristocracy, would be stereotyped, and might more properly be called castes?

Harington. Yes. As I was saying the other day, the general type of Aristocracy has been drawn, once and for all, by Plato; the details, of course, must vary according to time and place.

Martin. Plato's classes were hereditary. Do you accept that?

Harington. Certainly.

Martin. And do you approve also his regulations for the breeding of citizens?

Harington. Some such regulations there would have to be, if an ideal Aristocracy were to be established. For it must be possible to know, generally speaking,

(2) Aristocracy

what faculties every child who is born possesses, and to what class he naturally belongs; and to secure that in each class only the right number of people is born.

Martin. I see. Your ideal then is that of Plato, a system of caste, but one perfectly ordered, so that every man has from his birth a function assigned to him exactly correspondent to his faculties, and also necessary to the Good of the whole community; that Good, and not the particular interest of the governing class, being the end for which the society exists.

Harington. Precisely; and such a Society Plato called just, defining Justice as the performance by each class of its appropriate function, and the absence of any usurpation of the functions of one by another.

(3) Ochlocracy

Martin. You accept, then, in general, Plato's account of Aristocracy. And do you also endorse his description of Democracy?

Harington. Yes; I define Democracy as the rule of the Mass. The superiorities and inferiorities on which Aristocracy rests it ignores. Merit it denies or suppresses. Its only standard is numbers; and numbers it supposes to be composed of identical units which it calls average men. It admits no classes, no distinctions, no subordination. In its ultimate and most logical form it refers everything to the lot; and is really not a polity at all, but, as many now maintain, an Anarchy.

Martin. You follow Plato very faithfully. But one

thing I must ask: is Democracy, so described, a type or an actuality? **(3) Ochlocracy**

Harington. It's a type, if you like; but it typifies all democratic states.

Martin. Well, first let me get at the essence of the type. Is it the denial by Democracy of all special capacity, so that to any office it is as willing to appoint one person as another, and in all important decisions prefers to consult the average man, rather than professed experts?

Harington. That is part of my indictment; but further I hold that Democracy, besides denying superiorities of capacity, denies also superiorities of value. It does not hold one object or activity to be intrinsically better than another; and in particular does not value culture or art or science, except so far as science may be capable of utilitarian applications.

Martin. I see. Democracy, in your view, is not only government by the mass of men; but also by a mass that has no standards.

Harington. Yes.

Martin. Well, I do not deny that in actual democracies, so far as we have experience of them—and we have very little—there does exist, among others, the tendency you describe. But a Society in which such tendencies really predominated I should prefer not to call democratic. I want to reserve the word Democracy for my ideal, as you have the word Aristocracy for yours. I

3 **Ochlocracy** will not therefore accept as the definition of Democracy the rule of a Mass that has no standards. Such a Society I regard, like Oligarchy, as the perversion of an ideal; and I propose, if you will allow me, to name it Ochlocracy.

Harington. Name it as you please. But then, what is the ideal which you would call democratic?

Martin. I will come to that in a moment. But first let me suggest that Oligarchy and Ochlocracy are perversions that mutually engender each other. For when the standards set are class-standards, or are distorted and exploited by class-prejudice, there will be, naturally, on the part of the mass of men, a reaction against all standards. If culture and art and science are class-privileges, the odium that attaches to class will attach also to them; and those who are excluded from the privilege will view the accomplishment itself with the same jealousy and hatred which attaches to those who possess it. And similarly, if administrative and political capacity are the heritage of a governing class, ruling principally in their own interests, then that capacity itself will become sinister and odious to those who are its victims rather than its beneficiaries. Ochlocracy, so far as it has existed, has always been a reaction against Oligarchy; and we ought not to make it the measure of the possibilities of Democracy.

Harington. But once more, what do you understand by Democracy?

Martin. I am coming to that now; and it will be easier for me to describe the ideal now that we have discriminated its perversion. First, Democracy, in my view, would be distinguished from Ochlocracy by the fact that it would have standards, and right standards. On all important points it might refer the decision to the mass; but the mass would be composed of enlightened individuals, not of ignorant, jealous and small-minded units. And, further, while it would not aim at special capacity, neither would it ignore it, but would endeavour always to put the most capable man in his proper place, and respect and trust him according to his capacity. (4) **Democracy**

Harington. You are describing something very like what I call Aristocracy.

Martin. The distinction, however, is important. Aristocracy, as you conceive it, is hierarchic. It is divided into fixed classes, and those classes are arranged in a descending scale, from the highest, or governing class, downward. Its order is one of subordination, of inferior and superior; so that all the higher functions are entrusted permanently to a certain caste, and the lower and lowest to other castes. That is your conception, is it not?

Harington. Yes.

Martin. But in Democracy as I conceive it, there is nothing of all that. There would be different functions, but not different classes, still less castes. Above all,

(4) Democracy

there would be no governing class, though there might be trained administrative officials. So far as possible all citizens would receive an equally high standard of education, and be competent to perform equally high functions. In any case, difference of capacity would not involve difference of social rank; and the principle of the society would be a co-ordination of equals rather than a subordination of unequals. Democracy, in a word, would establish equality of status without identity of function, and popular control without confusion of standards. It would thus be distinguished both from Aristocracy and from Ochlocracy; and, of course, it could not be confused with Oligarchy. Will that do for a first outline?

Harington. Yes, but it wants a great deal of filling in.

Stuart. So, if I may say so, do the other types proposed.

Martin. No doubt; but one must begin somewhere, and I have the pedantry of the professor. I like to proceed methodically.

Stuart. Well, go on. I do not want to interrupt.

(5) Existing Society

Martin. I shall try not to abuse your patience; and perhaps the next step will interest you more. For I want now to describe, in relation to the four types we have distinguished, the actual society in which we are living, and around which, of course, our whole interest really centres.

Stuart. Here, then, is where I come in.

Martin. You will come in, I hope, wherever you feel inclined. (5) **Existing Society**

Stuart. Thank you. Pray then, continue.

Martin. I will begin by asking Harington to which of the four types he would liken our society.

Harington. I should say it is in a transitional stage between Oligarchy and Ochlocracy. In the eighteenth century it was wholly oligarchic; the landed gentry governed, and governed in their own interest.

Stuart. Did they? I thought they laid the foundations of the empire.

Harington. I admit that, like most Oligarchies, they were aggressive and predatory. But they were none the less an Oligarchy, according to our definition. For their fundamental principle of government was the maintenance of their own power.

Stuart. Yes; and they deserved the power they maintained. They had an ideal of personal honour; they had courage, force, and initiative; and they had, what I should have thought you would value, good taste and good manners, and a respect for philosophy, art and science.

Harington. I think it is true that some of them had. When you come to concrete cases, no society can be expected to correspond exactly to any simple type; and I should admit that most Oligarchies have had some aristocratic qualities. But, whatever may have been the position in the eighteenth century, everything

(5) **Existing Society** is altered now. With the loss of responsibility and power, which I date from 1832, our oligarchs, or aristocrats, if you like, have been losing also their character. They no longer impose standards of honour, of public spirit, or of taste; and the only people whose respect they command are publicans, flunkeys and spinsters.

Stuart. O come! You must in fairness admit that some of our most capable statesmen are still drawn from the Aristocracy.

Harington. I grant it; but they are survivals; they do not represent the real trend of our Society. That, I am sure, is now ochlocratic; for I must not, after Martin's definition, call it democratic. The principle we have established, or are establishing, is that of Number. Number determines the policy of our government, the character of our education, the direction of our social and national ethics. Are we to be drunk or sober? We ask the majority. Are we to be an empire or an island-state? We ask the majority. Are we to study Latin and Greek, or shorthand and book-keeping? We ask the majority. Is our language to be a choice instrument of thought or a vulgar and indistinguished dialect? We ask the majority. The "hundred best books," the best play of the season, the most competent soldier, the most distinguished statesman—all these points we refer to the majority. Numbers rule us; and numbers composed not of Martin's democratic individuals, but of the casual, untrained, characterless units of Ochlocracy. (5) **Existing Society**

Stuart. I'm sorry to pull you up, but that, again, seems to me an exaggeration. There are plenty of men of character left, at any rate in Scotland.

Martin. Perhaps we have a few even in England.

Stuart. Oh, England I leave to your tender mercies.

Martin. I am afraid I can't altogether defend it against the charge of Ochlocracy; but what strikes me even more is its oligarchic character. Harington suggests that Oligarchy is disappearing; I should say that it is changing its form, from an Oligarchy of birth to an Oligarchy of wealth; and that what he calls Ochlocracy is, in part, only the masque under which the transformation is being accomplished. It is not really numbers that rule, but that which controls numbers. And what is that? At every point, wealth. Modern Society, as I see it, from top to bottom, is a descending hierarchy of oligarchic groups, each with its own peculiar privileges, for which it fights and in and by which it lives. I image society as a pyramid, broadening down from its apex in a series of steps, each cut off from the one above, not indeed by an impassable barrier, but by a height which it requires a considerable degree of athleticism to scale; and on each step, crowded together, a fighting, trampling mob of desperate men, bent, every one, above all, on enlarging his own space and making room for his children, under penalty,

(5) **Existing Society** if he fails, that he or they will be thrust down to the step below, and perhaps, through all the degrees, to the very bottom. So that they are bound, all of them, at every stage, to make as difficult as possible access from the stage below, by maintaining and enhancing the privileges that protect their own area, whether they be members of a profession, like the Bar, or bankers, or University dons, or skilled artisans, or whatever it may be;—to maintain and to raise the standard of living of their class is the chief object, and to narrow the gate by which outsiders try to hustle in, by limiting the number of people who can obtain the requisite training, and in any other way that may be possible diminishing competition. And this conduct, surely, and this attitude of mind, is through and through oligarchic?

Stuart. How violent you philosophers are! I hardly recognise in your description the decent orderly society in which we all live.

Martin. Nothing is harder to perceive than the element one breathes. But I think a visitor descending among us from the upper air into these hollows and dens where we live and have our being, would see and judge us at least not less severely than I do. At any rate, that the oligarchic elements I have tried to disentangle are really to be found among us, whatever may be their proportion to the whole,—that, I am sure, is indisputable.

Harington. I admit the Oligarchy.

Martin. And I admitted the Ochlocracy. But do you see also any elements that are aristocratic? **(5) Existing Society**

Harington. I conceded to Stuart certain survivals from an earlier régime. But these are rapidly disappearing, and do not really count.

Martin. And I, on the other hand, perceive certain elements which are perhaps the beginnings of a Democracy; such as free compulsory education, and competitive examinations, and other measures and institutions tending to equalise opportunities and capacities. But these too are at present only rudiments. And, broadly, I should be inclined to describe our society as a fusion of the two perversions, Oligarchy and Ochlocracy.

Harington. I assent.

Martin. And, in this fusion, the two elements engender and intensify one another. For every privileged section, while it is oligarchic in relation to those below it, is ochlocratic in relation to those above. It despises and dreads its inferiors, and wants to keep them under; but of its superiors it is jealous and full of hate. Those privileges, it thinks, by which it is debarred from rising higher, are iniquitous and undeserved; those only by which it is prevented from sinking lower are legitimate and correspond to merit. Thus every class, while it maintains its own standard, disputes and denies the standard of those above it. The petty jealousy of Ochlocracy coexists with the narrow

(5) **Existing Society**

egotism of Oligarchy; and these two great serpents are eating one another, at every stage, from top to bottom of Society.

Stuart. I suppose I may put in a mild protest?

Martin. I beg your pardon, I was forgetting. Of course you do not agree with me. Tell me, then, where you think I am wrong.

Stuart. I don't say you're wrong; I don't see how one can be wrong or right in such a matter. You see the thing from one angle, and I from another. You regard it as a perversion of an ideal, and say "How bad it is!" I regard it as a product of the Real and say, "How much worse it might be!" I don't dispute your facts, I dispute your emphasis.

Martin. And that dispute, again, goes back to the one we started with. If I judge society hardly, that is because I believe that some at least of its defects are due to conditions which we can alter. You believe the contrary, and therefore are more inclined to leniency. So that really it would be waste of time for us to develop our differences at this point. If I am to convert you at all, I must be able to show that by maintaining certain institutions which we might alter, we perpetuate certain evils which we might cure. Do you agree? And may I continue on those lines?

Stuart. By all means, do.

§ 3. **The Institution of Marriage**

Martin. What, then, I will ask now, are the really important institutions?

A POLITICAL DIALOGUE

The Institution of Marriage

Stuart. The most important, I suppose, is Government.

Martin. The political philosophers seem to think so, and perhaps they were not very wrong, so long as government was in the hands of a King or a caste, and no reform in institutions could be accomplished except by a political revolution. Still, even then, what really gave its character to a society was not the form of its government, but the other institutions which the government supported. And since government has become, more or less, in most civilised states, a reflection of public opinion, it grows more and more obvious that it is not political but social institutions that really determine the character of the community.

Stuart. What do you mean by social institutions?

Martin. I mean especially those great fly-wheels that control the whole machine, the institutions of marriage and of property.

Stuart. Marriage?

Martin. Yes; shall we begin with that?

Stuart. Is there much to say about it?

Martin. Much too much! Only it is so difficult to say.

Stuart. Property, I can understand, from your point of view, is important; but why marriage? In any society, I should have thought, however it might otherwise be constituted, marriage would be arranged much as it is now.

Martin. Possibly; but it is not obvious, and I want

The Institution of Marriage

to consider the matter freely, as though it were an open question.

Stuart. Well, it seems curious; but I have no objection.

Martin. What then is marriage, from the social point of view? It is the mechanism, is it not, which controls the production and rearing of children?

Stuart. Yes, I suppose so.

Martin. Its importance then is obvious; for upon it depend the number and the quality of the population.

Stuart. Yes; but that's a matter that must be left to the parents.

Martin. We must not dismiss the question so quickly and so easily as that. Whether, in the last resort, it must be left to the parents may be considered later. But some discussion we must have first as to what ought to be aimed at, whether by parents or by public authority.

Stuart. Well, proceed.

(1) On regulating the number of the population

Martin. And first, as to numbers. Is it not to you a very curious thing that the pulpit and the press and the politicians always assume, as though it were a self-evident axiom, that any check in the rate of increase of population is an evil, and that a stationary or declining birth-rate means national decadence?

Stuart. Well, doesn't it?

Martin. Not obviously, or necessarily, so far as I can see. What is desirable, I suppose, from an economic point of view, is that measure of population which is most productive, given the existing technical and other conditions. If the population is less or greater than that, you get less wealth per head. And if the disproportion becomes very great you may reach the starvation point.

(1) On regulating the number of the population

Stuart. That bugbear of Malthus I thought was discredited.

Martin. I do not believe it to be a bugbear, I believe it to be a real wild beast, that has devoured its thousands and millions in the past. And if we, in the West, during the last century or so, owing to quite exceptional conditions, have been able to keep it at bay, yet is it not, even now, ravaging elsewhere? It looks, at any rate, as though in India and China the population tends to multiply beyond the limit of subsistence, and is only kept within it by the intervention of famine and plague.

Stuart. That is because modern methods of industry have not yet been fully applied in those countries.

Martin. Possibly; and it may happen—no one, I suppose, can tell—that we shall so multiply and perfect our means of controlling nature that the danger of population outstripping subsistence may become and remain negligible all over the world. But, even so, that would not be all we want. We want, surely, if society is to advance as we all desire, a much higher average standard of well-being than now prevails even

(1) On regulating the number of the population

in the West. And that, I suppose, might involve—I don't know whether it would—a considerable reduction of population. The question is very technical and I do not pretend to dogmatise about it. Only I insist that the aim of society should be not a large population at all costs, but the largest compatible with the highest level of civilisation throughout the whole community.

Stuart. That might be all very well for an isolated nation; but it does not allow for the struggle between races. For example, if the West doesn't increase its population in the same proportion as the East, it is bound to go under in the competition.

Martin. Why? Efficiency in such contests tells far more than numbers. Did numbers help Russia or China to conquer Japan? Do numbers help the Indians to overthrow the British rule? Has not a minority everywhere, always, dominated the world? Poor, uneducated, unintelligent masses are no strength to any community.

Stuart. Perhaps not. But even supposing it were desirable to limit numbers, how do you propose to do it?

Martin. It is doing itself before our eyes. In the upper and middle classes, and among the more intelligent artisans, parents do actually now fix the number of children they will have, in proportion to their resources. And so far, and on the face of it, that is a thing to be commended.

(1) On regulating the number of the population

Stuart. As often as not, I believe, it is the result of sheer selfishness in the parents.

Martin. There may be selfish motives at work, as well as others, but that does not affect the desirability of the result. And for my part, if you speak of selfishness, I can imagine nothing more selfish than to bring children into the world without any consideration as to whether or how one will be able to provide adequately for them.

Stuart. How does one ever know? I believe those things ought to be left to settle themselves.

Martin. It is the doctrine of the pulpit; but tor my part I do not believe in throwing our responsibilities on Providence. The man I respect is the man who does his best to forecast the contingencies of the future, especially in such an important matter as the introduction of children into the world without their own consent.

Stuart. Well, I don't see how you can do it.

Martin. The fact remains that people do do it; and for my part I commend them for it.

Stuart. But what is the consequence? The best people, or at any rate the most prudent and far-sighted, restrict their numbers, and the poor and improvident do not; so that you get a population continually declining in quality. That is the immediate result of all this calculation and forethought!

Martin. Not of the calculation and forethought, but

(1) On regulating the number of the population

of the lack of it among all the lower strata of society. The moral, surely, is that the practice of the upper classes should be extended to the lower. And, from that point of view, is not the intervention of authority to prevent the spread of knowledge upon this subject one of the most extraordinary examples of interference against the public good which even the history of governments can furnish?

Stuart. That follows, I suppose, from your argument. But this whole business of limiting families remains revolting to me.

Martin. I understand your feeling. But, really, have we any right to indulge our feelings in the matter? It is the welfare of children and of the community that is at stake. And surely, from that, the most important point of view, we ought to welcome the widest possible diffusion among parents of a sense of responsibility and of a knowledge of how to make the responsibility effective?

Stuart. You can't guarantee that the knowledge will not be misused, as it clearly often is, to evade the responsibilities of parentage.

Martin. All knowledge is a double-edged tool; but we have no other. And I think you would really agree that we must spread light and take the risks.

(2) On regulating the quality of the population

Stuart. I suppose so. But, at best, what knowledge have we to spread? Far more important, I suppose, than the number of the population is its quality. From the point of view we are now taking, marriages clearly,

I suppose, ought to be arranged with a view to the excellence of the children who are to be born of them. But even if we wished it, could we effectively do anything of the kind? Do we know how?

(2) On regulating the quality of the population

Martin. The first condition of acquiring knowledge is to desire it. And on this point society, I think, has never really desired it. The ancient world, it is true, cared more about the question than the modern world has done up to now. Their thinkers were well aware that the main determinant in the marriage relation ought to be the quality of the offspring; and they had methods, very rough and ready no doubt, of trying to attain the object. Christianity and the Middle Ages meant a retrogression in this as in so many other matters. And though the writers of the Renaissance revived the idea, it has never influenced the minds of the mass of men.

Stuart. Would men, in any case, ever allow institutions to interfere in such a matter?

Martin. They have always allowed them to interfere, and to interfere drastically. But the extraordinary thing is—it really is extraordinary when you come to reflect upon it—that the restrictions imposed do not seem commonly to have had any reference to the most important purpose served by marriage. They have sometimes been suggested by the customs or laws of the devolution of property, sometimes apparently by pure superstitions to us quite unintelligible, sometimes

(2) On regulating the quality of the population

by a kind of metaphysical logic; but I doubt whether they have ever been framed with a view to the production of the best children; and many of them probably could not be maintained on that ground even though they may be otherwise desirable. The much debated question of marriage with a deceased wife's sister is only one example of what I mean.

Stuart. It's curious.

Martin. It really is very curious. I doubt whether anyone, if he were challenged offhand, could say what the reasons are for the prohibitions we now accept without question. There may be very good reasons, in some cases clearly there are. But it is a remarkable testimony to our lack of reflection on these subjects that our rules are never revised, or even challenged, except in the one instance I have just mentioned. And while we thus unquestioningly accept certain prohibitions because they are traditional, we have hardly begun to ask ourselves whether there are not others far more important which we ought to introduce. Criminals, lunatics, syphilitic and phthisical people, any and every one may marry, so long as they are without the prohibited degrees, and may produce as many children as they like, without any consideration as to whether or no they are handing on to posterity their own vices and diseases.

Stuart. That is, no doubt, very regrettable; but I don't see how you can stop it.

Martin. The conditions of stopping it are first, knowledge, and secondly, will; or, perhaps I should say, first, will, and secondly, knowledge. If society is to progress, this, I believe, is one of the problems with which it must be most preoccupied; and with the development of knowledge we may expect that there will come a development in the institution of marriage on the lines of prohibiting, whether by law or opinion or both, unions which it is known will result in bad offspring, and encouraging those which will result in good. That, at any rate, is a cautious statement; and so far, I hope, I have carried you with me?

(2) On regulating the quality of the population

Stuart. I don't object to the suggestion, but it's altogether impracticable. Men will never submit to any interference in such matters.

Martin. On the contrary, there has never yet been a Society in which people have not submitted to the extreme of interference, if not by law then by opinion. In savage societies innumerable restrictions on marriage, to modern inquirers meaningless and unintelligible, are constantly found to exist and to be effectually enforced; and in civilised communities such considerations as rank and property have always been, and still often are, paramount in the formation of unions. In how many countries, and in how many families, is a woman really free to accept or reject a husband? In how many, really, does a man choose his wife simply on the score of his inclination? And if all these social and family

(3) On the possibility of such regulation

(3) On the possibility of such regulation restrictions, often stupid or merely egoistic, can be successfully imposed, is it unreasonable to hope that an intelligent Society would submit to regulations known and understood to be made in the public interest?

Stuart. But even granting that the restrictions might be made effective, I see all sorts of other difficulties. In the first place, it is so hard to say what you want to breed for. Do you want, for instance, a number of narrowly specialised types, some intellectual, some physical, and so on, or do you want a high average type?

Martin. The answer to that question must depend on the kind of Society you have in view, a point to which we shall come directly. But meantime, in any cases we may surely say this much, that even if it were hard to determine what types should be included, it should not be hard to determine what should be ruled out. When disease, mental or physical, is known to be hereditary, then, at least, the begetting and bearing of children should be forbidden. For even that small beginning we should be thankful; and from it much might follow as experience developed and ideals became clearer.

Stuart. Well, let us grant that, if you like. But still there is the further difficulty which we have already touched upon, that even if we knew what to breed for, we don't know how to do it. The Ancients, as I understand from what you said, made a great point of regulating marriage with a view to good offspring; but did they have any satisfactory notion as to the means whereby the end can be attained?

(3) On the possibility of such regulation

Martin. They had a kind of rough empiricism which satisfied them more easily, no doubt, than it should have done; though there was more hope of progress in their attitude than in our own, because they did at least recognise that the end was one which Society ought to keep in view, even if they were ignorant as to the means; whereas we do not even admit the end. Only in quite recent years have a few bold men, like Francis Galton, ventured to assert the importance of breeding for a good stock, and initiated the inquiries that may lead to knowledge on the subject. But I, for my part, have sufficient faith in science to believe that once men really want to do the thing, they will find out how to do it. The advance of science is due as much to a favourable social environment as to individual genius and patience; and once our idle and pernicious prejudice is broken down, that the production of children is a private and irresponsible function, we may hope that along with the desire to find the true method of breeding, will be developed also the necessary knowledge.

(4) On Love and Marriage

Stuart. Even that I will admit to be possible, though I think the possibility very remote. But I have still another point which I am half afraid to introduce into this grave discussion. Still, I'm a Scot, and all Scots are at heart sentimentalists; and what I want to know is this. In proportion as it becomes the custom or

(4) **On Love and Marriage** the law that marriages shall be arranged exclusively with reference to the likelihood of good offspring, the practice of marrying for love, I suppose, must decline. What then—you will think the question very trifling,—what is to happen to love?

Martin. A trifling question do you expect me to think it? As though anything could be trifling which deals with love! If indeed, by love you mean that unaccountable passion, of all things the most mysterious, the most terrible, and the most divine, whereby bodies and souls are drawn to one another in defiance of all other affinities, be they interests or occupations or convictions, by an impulse so profound that it seems to have its source beyond the portals of life, so imperative that it overrides every other tie, so instinctive that it sweeps Reason like dust before its onset. You mean, I suppose, the Eros of the Greeks, the irresistible god, not Cupid or Venus nor any of the lighter loves with which a man may dally but to which, if he is wise and sane, he will not succumb?

Stuart. I mean any kind of personal attraction, such as commonly precedes and leads on to marriage.

Martin. But such attractions, as they are commonly felt, are not so fatally and irretrievably fixed on a single person that they may not be diverted, without serious trouble or loss, if their first object should prove, for some reason or another, to be unattainable. Most men, and most women, are capable, are they not, of "falling in love," as it is called, with a considerable number of people; and it would be hard if, in a well-ordered society, it were not as practicable as it is in our own, to combine this kind of love with marriage. For even now, as we agreed, most, or at least very many marriages are determined by other considerations, primarily, than those of passion; and these, experience shows, are not the least happy unions. The love that is important for marriage is rather that which comes after than that which precedes, the sincere and sober affection which results from a common life and common responsibilities.

(4) **On Love and Marriage**

Stuart. That may be all very true, but it doesn't meet my difficulty. There is a kind of love which is important for its own sake, and ought not to be subordinated to any other purpose. When people feel that passion, it is for the sake of the union that they want to unite. If children result, that is a mere accident from the point of view of their purpose; and whether or no children result, and whatever the quality of the children, the union is a thing demanded by their personality, and its prohibition is the greatest and most unendurable of tyrannies.

Martin. You touch a point of real difficulty, not only for an imaginary society, but for any which actually exists. For though I believe that, in most cases, such love as people are capable of feeling is readily enough diverted into channels where it may find its satisfaction

(4) On Love and Marriage

in matrimony, yet I admit the exceptions, and they may be of a kind which, whatever the order of Society, must inevitably lead to tragedy. There is such a thing as the great passion, the passion of the poets and of Plato; though it is, I am inclined to think, much rarer than is commonly supposed. It is often confused, by sentimental men and women, with the mere yearnings of unsatisfied desire; but when it exists it is, and it should be, sole and indisputable lord of those whom it inspires. But being, of all the powers of the world, the most capricious and irrational, it may easily fasten upon objects of pursuit the most unattainable, or, from some other point of view, the most undesirable. Not only may it meet with no return where it has fixed its desires, but a thousand obstacles, approved by reason, may intervene to bar the union it seeks. That is so, and always has been so, in actual societies, as is witnessed by all the tragedies of love. And it need not be more so, though I will not say it would be less, in the better ordered community we are imagining. For the only test such a community would impose would concern the fitness of the pair to produce offspring. If that test were passed there might result that rarest and sweetest of all relationships, where a strong personal passion is perpetuated and reinforced by a joint participation in the chances of life and the care of children. But even if that were forbidden, the pair might live their life together, in a relationship beautiful, faithful, and profound even if not perfect. The society I am imagining would indeed be more, not less free than our own; for its public opinion would be more tolerant and more sane. It is not love but parentage that would be restricted; and that only in the well-understood and reasonable interest of the community. And ought such restraint really to be regarded as a tyranny? (4) **On Love and Marriage**

Stuart. Perhaps it ought not, but I think it would be.

Martin. Well, I must be satisfied with that; and now, perhaps, we may return to the point you raised, and I postponed, as to what kind of types we ought to breed for. I postponed it because it is one on which, I imagine, Harington and I must disagree; and I wanted first to get out conclusions which I supposed would be common to us both. I don't know whether I have succeeded; Harington has been very silent.

Harington. I don't think I have dissented on any important point. But I confess that I have been rather distracted with considering how I should arrange this matter in an Aristocracy. (5) **On the breeding of types in an Aristocracy**

Martin. Well, we are now coming to that. And that we may isolate the problem, I must ask Stuart to permit me the preposterous assumption that we have the knowledge and the will to breed for what types we choose, and that the only real question is what types we do choose.

Stuart. If you admit that the assumption is preposterous I am content to let you make it.

(5) On the breeding of types in an Aristocracy

Martin. Well then, we can start. And I shall ask Harington, who has been meditating on the subject all this time, what an Aristocracy would breed for.

Harington. I see no way out of the conclusion that it must breed for specialised quality. Its form being, as we defined it, a hierarchy of fixed classes, where function corresponds to aptitude, it would endeavour to secure that each class should reproduce the proper number of its own kind, artisans artisans, traders traders, rulers rulers, and so on.

Martin. On this point, too, then, you follow Plato?

Harington. Logic compels me. But what has been troubling me is, that I cannot dismiss, as he did, the whole of the working-class as hardly deserving the attention of a philosopher. I imagine myself dealing with a complex industrial organisation of the modern type, and that forces upon me the question whether, if such an organisation were aristocratically controlled, specialisation in breeding would not have to be as minute as specialisation in industry.

Martin. You mean you would have to breed one class, say, for folding paper, another for stitching, another for pasting, and so on; or one for each of the processes that go to make a pin, and so throughout?

Harington. That's the kind of thing. Of course I don't really think that, even in an Aristocracy, specialisation need be as minute as that. Still, if my fundamental condition is to be carried out, and function is to correspond exactly to aptitude, the specialisation of types will be, at any rate, rather complicated.

(5) **On the breeding of types in an Aristocracy**

Martin. I think it will. And for that reason, among others, perhaps an aristocratic organisation would be less well suited to a community of the modern type than to the Platonic City-State. However, it would be pedantic to press you for details. I understand that the ideal of Aristocracy is specialisation, and that it would aim nowhere at a complete man, but everywhere at men with some peculiar and perhaps very minute aptitude?

Harington. Some at least of its citizens would be much more complete than are to be met with in actual societies. The higher the class, the wider and the more human would be its activity; and the class of rulers, like Plato's philosophers, would embrace the whole range of knowledge and accomplishment, being at once statesmen, thinkers and artists, or at least connoisseurs.

Martin. I understand. At the top of Society would be men so complete, in character and mind, as to realise the whole range of the human ideal; and at the bottom men of the most minutely specialised aptitudes and outlooks. The upper classes would be greater and nobler than they are among us; and the lower smaller and more ignoble?

Harington. If the latter were possible!

Martin. Perhaps it might not only be possible, but necessary to the aristocratic ideal. But now, to con-

(5) **On the breeding of types in an Aristocracy**

trast with this the ideal of Democracy. Democracy, as I conceive it, would breed not for specialisation, but for a high average of capacity.

(6) **On the breeding of types in a Democracy**

Harington. But occupations must surely be specialised as much in Democracy as in Aristocracy.

Martin. Not so much, or so rigidly, I think. Indeed, it might be the aim of the society to encourage as much variation of employment as would be compatible with efficiency. But in any case, the Democracy I conceive would not aim at specialised faculty, it would aim at the all-round man. For it would hold that work is for the sake of life, not life for the sake of work, and that the best part of life is not that which is spent in necessary, but often uncongenial and narrowing, work, but that which is employed at will in free leisure. My Democracy, then, would breed for general ability, such as could turn readily to anything and perform anything efficiently. The complete man, as opposed to the specialist, would be its aim; and its task, I think, for that reason would be easier than that of Aristocracy, because what it would mainly have to do would be to eliminate the unfit, a far simpler problem than that of positively creating an indefinite number of highly specialised types.

Harington. I admit that, when one comes to work it out, this business of breeding seems the most paradoxical element in an Aristocracy.

Martin. My own idea is that, apart from all practical

difficulties, it is the rock upon which Aristocracy as an ideal goes to pieces. But that point we will leave till the time has come to compare our positions. Meantime, from this rather inconclusive discussion, it does seem to emerge that if ever there is to be a well-ordered community it must learn to control its population, whether by law or by opinion, or in whatever way may be most effective; and that the existing haphazard arrangements are altogether unsatisfactory, even though, because of our ignorance and our prejudices, they may be at present inevitable. And, further, it is clear, I think, that the kind of type for which a society having the requisite will and knowledge should breed, will be determined by its general ideal. So that a criticism of ideals has a very real and practical significance. Will even Stuart go so far with us?

(6) On the breeding of types in a Democracy

Stuart. Yes. So long as you remain in the air I have no difficulty in following you.

Martin. It is most desirable, then, that we should continue to fly. But I am afraid that will be more difficult in pursuing the very pedestrian subject to which we must now turn in order.

Stuart. That is property, I suppose.

§ 4. The Institution of Property

Martin. Yes, property, that august and venerable institution, on which I almost fear to lay profane hands, so sacred is it, so powerful and so revered. For is it not a god, the only one left upon earth; and is not the law its temple, which it is sacrilege to profane?

The Institution of Property

Stuart. You are wasting your irony upon me; I am not to be provoked.

Martin. And yet there is a look in your eye which warns me to go carefully. However, I cannot turn back; and so, to give myself courage and to propitiate you, I will begin by reminding us both of the extraordinary importance of this institution, and the absolute necessity laid upon us to deal courageously with it.

Stuart. I do not need convincing of that.

Martin. Let me, nevertheless, set it out in form.

Stuart. Proceed then.

Martin. Marriage, we saw, determines the original character and aptitude of the citizen; but property determines his opportunities. And the two together, so far as social factors are concerned, determine the whole course of his life. Whether a man must work, whether he is to be permitted to work, or whether he is to be dispensed from the necessity of working; and again, at what he is to work, whether at manual labour or at one of the professions, whether at a skilled or an unskilled employment, whether at an art, or a handicraft, or a mechanical routine; all this is governed by the amount of property owned by his parents or himself. And again, the remuneration he is to receive for his labour is fixed by the same condition. Either he has access to well-paid or to ill-paid work; and the access, though it depends partly on natural capacity, depends still more, in practice, on opportunity.

Broadly speaking, the sons of the rich remain rich, and the sons of the poor remain poor, though of course the exceptions are numerous and important. So that the whole system of classes in any society is determined by the institution of property interacting with the institution of marriage. Are there idle classes? Are there criminal classes? Are there classes of unemployed and unemployable? Are there classes living at the verge of starvation, and liable, at the least disturbance, to be shaken down among the paupers or the criminals? Are there others so rich that their whole life is one long process of demoralisation both of themselves and of those with whom they come into contact? For all this, the institution of property is responsible. And upon these factors, again, depends the whole order of the society, its stability or instability, its progress or stagnation, its harmony or its dissonance. So that, one may fairly say, the character of any community is completely determined, in all essential points, by the joint operation of the institutions of marriage and property.

The Institution of Property

Stuart. You seem to attribute to the institution of property a great deal which I should attribute to the activities of men.

Martin. Because these activities are limited and defined in their scope and results by the institution. If, for example, a man inherits wealth, that is because of the law of property; and if he did not inherit, his whole life would be different. If, again, he lives upon

The Institution of Property

rent, that is because of the law of property; and if all rent belonged to the community, his whole life would be different. It is the law that determines in what things there shall be property, and under what conditions; whether property may be transferred and under what forms. And to those rules the whole activity of society adjusts itself.

Stuart. But those rules are necessary.

Martin. In what sense? They have come to seem to us necessary because we are used to them. But are they necessary in themselves?

Stuart. When I call them necessary, I mean that, in my belief, they are the only rules that will work.

Martin. I am not prepared to admit that. I agree however, of course, that our rules do work, only they seem to me to work very curiously.

Stuart. How so?

Martin. I am going to explain. Broadly speaking there are two things which are governed by the law of property,—interacting always, as we presuppose, with the law of marriage. The first is the distribution of labour among the members of the community; the second, the distribution of the products of labour. These two points, of course, are intimately connected; for, so far as a choice is open, that kind of labour will tend to be chosen which provides the highest remuneration. Still, it will be convenient for our purpose to take them separately.

(1) The distribution of labour in Existing Society

Stuart. How do you mean that the distribution of labour is determined by the law of property?

Martin. I mean only the obvious fact, that the labour which is best remunerated and most coveted, that of the professions and of the higher posts in business, is far more accessible, if not exclusively accessible, to the sons of the rich and of the well-to-do than to others. It requires, to begin with, an elaborate and expensive education; and even if that be dispensed with, relationship and social connexion count for much. Those who have means are more or less sharply cut off from those who have not; they have among one another a kind of freemasonry; and they naturally incline, wherever they can, to confer lucrative and interesting posts, if not upon their own immediate relations and friends, at least upon members of their own class.

Stuart. I think you exaggerate that tendency. In business, at any rate, men are always rising from the bottom to the top.

Martin. They do rise, no doubt; but in what numbers and in what percentage? Exceptional ability, even where opportunity is scanty, will, I freely admit, make a career for itself even in Europe, and still more in new countries. But for the ordinary man of average powers, it is opportunity that determines his fate; and opportunity is the monopoly of the well-to-do. It follows that since the well-to-do are a small minority, the great mass of men are predestined to the less interesting,

(1) The distribution of labour in Existing Society

more laborious, and worse remunerated kinds of labour. Normally, the sons of manual labourers become manual labourers, or, at best, or worst, clerks; the sons of clerks, clerks; the sons of shop-keepers, shop-keepers, and so on, up the scale. Or, if the son does not actually follow his father's occupation, he follows one of similar grade, or, perhaps, one grade higher or lower. If the son of a waiter becomes a barrister, or the son of a gardener a physician, that is a matter for surprise and comment. Our society in effect, and subject, I admit, to numerous exceptions, is a society of hereditary classes; and it is so because of the institution of property.

Stuart. The institution of property is a very vague phrase. What exact point in our system are you attacking?

Martin. Clearly the point in question here is the law of inheritance and bequest. If the property of the father did not normally descend to the son, little if little, and much if much, then, though there might be a stratification of society, the stratification would not be hereditary. Everybody might then start with more or less equal opportunities; and the position reached would be really determined in each case by natural aptitude.

Stuart. I don't see how that could be worked out.

Martin. It is not my present business to say how it

might be worked out, but to point out the effects of the existing arrangement. It results, you will perhaps agree, broadly speaking, in a society of hereditary classes. And so far we have something like Harington's Aristocracy.

(1) The distribution of labour in Existing Society

Harington. I protest. The distinction is far more important than the resemblance. For in an Aristocracy, as I defined it, the classes would correspond to aptitudes. The carpenter would have the carpenter's talent, the mason the mason's, the clerk the clerk's, the physician the physician's, and so on, up to the governing class. Each citizen would really be fitted, and feel himself to be fitted, exactly for that work which he had to perform. All faculties would be employed to the best advantage, both for the individual and for the whole; so that the society would be as efficient and the members as contented, as it is possible to conceive. Whereas with us, all this is different. A man's position is not determined only by his aptitude, but also, and often more, by his fortune. He may have a genius for pure mathematics, for medicine, or for art, and yet be compelled to work as an unskilled labourer; or he may have no talent save his physical strength, and yet be a legislator in the House of Lords. His course of life is fixed by the position of his parents; and no machinery exists to adjust it to his capacities.

Stuart. Surely that is a great exaggeration. After all, I do not know that natural aptitude is very much

(1) The distribution of labour in Existing Society

specialised. My experience suggests to me that any man of average ability can do decently well almost any kind of work; the men of genius ear-marked for this or that pursuit are, I believe, very rare.

Martin. Even if that be true—and how true it is we are not in a position, I admit, to decide—it does not alter Harington's contention. For if we are to suppose most men to have a more or less equal all-round ability, then the selection of certain of them to perform the higher kinds of work, and of the great majority to perform the lower, is all the more clearly determined by the caprice of fortune, that is by the standing of their parents, not by any rational principle of equity or of efficiency. But in fact, even if natural ability be not highly specialised, experience surely shows that it differs in degree in different individuals. And we see every day, under our system, men of ridiculously inferior capacity filling high positions in Society, and men of great ability in circumstances where they have no scope to develop it.

Stuart. But the abler men are always rising to the top, the incompetent sinking to the bottom.

Martin. Granted, if you like; but this rising and sinking is so retarded by the institution of property that at any given moment in any generation the correspondence between function and capacity is of the slightest. So that I must still adhere, when all concessions have been made, to my original statement of the case. Our society, broadly speaking, is one of hereditary classes, determined not by aptitude, as would be the case in Aristocracy, but by wealth.

(1) The distribution of labour in Existing Society

Harington. In short, it is, as we agreed before, a form of Oligarchy.

Martin. Yes; and we can now say, more specifically, what form. For the position of the members, we see, is fixed almost entirely by their wealth, not as in some forms of Oligarchy, by their birth, noble or the reverse. In other words, our society is a Plutocracy.

Stuart. It is still so far aristocratic, or at least unplutocratic, that we have hereditary nobility.

Martin. We have, in England; but its importance is steadily declining, and is already measured rather by its wealth than by its rank. A nobleman, it is true, sits by right in the House of Lords; but he cannot hope to have much influence or weight unless he be also rich. England, like America, is a Plutocracy; and the same may be said of most European countries.

Harington. Most true; and that is why I find the modern world so mean.

Martin. Plutocracy, I agree, at its best is not a very noble form of society. But I am afraid we have not even got it at its best.

Stuart. How so?

Martin. The best form of Plutocracy, I suppose, would be one in which position and power would be apportioned not according to the mere possession of

(1) The distribution of labour in Existing Society

wealth, but according to the capacity to acquire and administer it.

Harington. Even so, Plutocracy, in my opinion, would be a bad thing. For the faculty of money-making, as far as I can see, is a kind of special gift, divorced from justice, humanity, benevolence, and even intelligence, in the larger and finer sense of the term; it is a sort of low cunning, combined with unscrupulousness; and to make this inferior instinct the main or only passport to power could never be a way of creating a just or harmonious or good society.

Martin. Still, it must be admitted that a community organised on that basis would at least be one where position would correspond to aptitude, even though the aptitude were a base one. But in our Society it is not the power to create or administer wealth, but the bare possession of it that confers position. And into possession of it men come by the most capricious and accidental ways, by inheritance, by gift, by lucky speculation, or what not. So that immense fortunes, over and over again, are owned and dissipated by men who could have never earned a penny; while others with great natural capacity for the manipulation of wealth never get an opportunity to make their talent tell. A Marquis of Anglesea is throwing away his millions whilst some village Carnegie or Rockefeller toils unrecognised at the plough or labours in the mine.

A POLITICAL DIALOGUE

Stuart. I don't much believe in the village Carnegie or Rockefeller. Such men nothing can keep down. (1) **The distribution of labour in Existing Society**

Martin. There is no doubt some truth in that; and so far as it is true, our society corresponds to the better type of Plutocracy.

Harington. Better! But what an indictment against any society, that the men who can't be kept down in it are just such men as that! Men, who in any decently organised community, would be put to the lowest and most menial tasks!

Stuart. Don't be too hard upon them! Even a millionaire may have his virtues. And, if I may venture to say so, I know men who have much money and who yet are not entirely devoid of intelligence and probity.

Harington. I beg your pardon! I know I am extravagant on this point. The vices of Plutocracy happen to be those which peculiarly exasperate me. But, of course, if one is to be reasonable, I admit that there are rich men who might be fit to rule even in an Aristocracy.

Stuart. I accept the handsome apology; but I will not accept without comment the description of our society as a Plutocracy. What strikes me about it is not the power of the rich, but the power of the masses. You see it not only in government, but in all economic relations. What do you make, for instance, of the action and the claims of Trades Unions?

(1) The distribution of labour in Existing Society

Martin. It is part of my contention that when you get Oligarchy you also get Ochlocracy. And in this connexion I not only admit, I insist upon the fact that where the mass of men are condemned, not on any principle of efficiency, but by sheer luck, to do the hardest and most disagreeable work, for the lowest remuneration, they will and must and do fall back upon the power of numbers as their only weapon and counterpoise. The principle on which classes are organised being radically defective, the necessary consequence is friction and discord. On the continent this situation has been frankly formulated by the Socialists as class-war. And if that formulation seems to Englishmen extreme and forced, it contains, for every country, at least so much truth that everywhere Society is in a position of unstable equilibrium. There is no balance or harmony, no recognition of equity, but a perpetual effort on the part of the poor to encroach upon the rich, and on the part of the rich to defend themselves against the poor. In our time, as much as in Plato's, every Society is divided if not into two, into many hostile camps; and for this division the institution of property is responsible.

Stuart. Well, it is the ochlocratic element, not the oligarchic one that I fear.

Martin. I fear both. But when you have Oligarchy, I hold it to be the only salvation that Ochlocracy should rise against it. From the clash of the two perhaps something better will result, if we will learn the lesson of the situation.

(1) The distribution of labour in Existing Society

Stuart. Why should it not be something worse that results?

Martin. It well may be, unless we learn to think and act rightly. And the first step to that is to see clearly what the present state of society is. I called it a Plutocracy, and you call it an Ochlocracy; but the truth, I think, is, as we said before, that it is both, the one constantly engendering the other. Will you accept that compromise?

Stuart. Provisionally, yes.

(2) The distribution of labour in an Aristocracy

Martin. Next, then, let us ask what we think would be a better order of society, so far as this point of the distribution of labour is concerned. And, as before, let us take first the aristocratic ideal, and ask Harington how he would arrange things if he had his way.

Harington. That I have already indicated. Aristocracy would be a system of hereditary classes; and so far would resemble our own Society. But these classes would be determined not by wealth, but by faculty; the existence of the requisite faculty in each class being guaranteed by a scientific plan of breeding. In other words, the distribution of labour among the members of the Society would be independent of property, and determined exclusively by the general interests of the community. Authority would decide that such and such classes of labourers were required, in such and

(2) The distribution of labour in an Aristocracy

such numbers; and provision would be made accordingly by those responsible for regulating marriage. The institution of property would have nothing to do with that matter; its only function would be the distribution of the rewards of labour.

Martin. That is what I imagined you would say; and I will only add a few words, for the sake of explicitness. Your classes would, of course, would they not, be more definite and fixed than they are in our Society?

Harington. Certainly. From the aristocratic point of view, the casual moving up and down from one class to another is a defect not a merit, a mere intrusion of anarchy.

Martin. And you would say the same, would you not, of the shifting of the classes themselves, the formation of new ones, as, recently, of the class of chauffeurs; the perpetual and incalculable emergence and disappearance of occupations, and of corresponding social strata, which is one of the noticeable features of modern industrial communities?

Harington. It is not so much the changes themselves, as their accidental character that would be repugnant to an Aristocracy. For I am not supposing, as Plato did, that my society would necessarily be stationary. I conceive it to be progressive; only the progress would be regulated and controlled by government. So that if new inventions, for example, led to new processes, and those to a demand for new classes of labour, then the processes would be introduced, and the labour provided by authority; the whole evolution thus remaining thoroughly under control, to the exclusion of all the disturbance, misery and disaster which is a normal feature of our own Societies.

(2) The distribution of labour in an Aristocracy

Martin. That is a new idea to me, that you conceive Aristocracy as progressive; and it differentiates your view fundamentally from that of Plato. It does not, however, affect the point which interests us for the moment, that, in an aristocratic community, all the higher functions, especially that of government, would be entrusted to a small hereditary minority?

Harington. Yes, that is so.

Martin. And all that we call culture, the appreciation, if not the practice of art, philosophy, literature and science, and the leisure and outlook necessary for such pursuits —all this would be the monopoly of the minority?

Harington. Yes; as it is with us, or rather would be, if those activities were seriously and nobly cultivated at all; and as it always has been wherever they have been cultivated.

Martin. And, on the other hand, the great mass of men, being specialised for mechanical and routine pursuits, would have neither the desire nor the faculty for the higher activities?

Harington. And not having either the desire or the faculty, they would of course feel no resentment at their exclusion.

(2) The distribution of labour in an Aristocracy

Martin. So that, in your view, though Aristocracy would be, if anything, more unequal than our own Society, it would nevertheless be more just. And being just, it would be harmonious; and being harmonious would be secure and stable?

Harington. Yes, that is my contention.

Martin. Well, I accept your description of the aristocratic ideal; and now, shall I go on to describe in turn my own ideal of Democracy, so far as this question of the distribution of labour is concerned?

Harington. Please do.

(3) The distribution of labour in a Democracy

Martin. First, in Democracy, as in Aristocracy, the distribution of labour would not be determined by the distribution of property, but by some other principle. I cannot, however, call in here the principle of Faculty. For, as we saw, Democracy would breed, not, like Aristocracy, for specialisation but for all-round capacity; and if it were successful in this, then, broadly speaking, any citizen so far as endowment is concerned, would be fit for any function, so that the actual function he is to perform and for which he is to be trained must be fixed by some other consideration.

Harington. By what, then?

Martin. By convenience. The citizens must be somehow induced and qualified to perform the work that is wanted, whatever be its character.

Stuart. I don't see then how Democracy would differ from our own society. For among us, too, presumably all work that is done is done because it is wanted by people who are fit to do it.

(3) The distribution of labour in a Democracy

Martin. The difference would lie in the character of the inducement offered. At present, all the disagreeable work gets done because the mass of people have no opportunity to do anything else; they must do it or starve. But in a Democracy, where there should be real equality of opportunity and approximate equality of capacity, there would have to be either some direct coercion upon every one to do his share of the onerous and necessary work; or else, some special inducement, in the way of wages or leisure, or honour, to attract men to otherwise unattractive labour. In any case, it would, I think, be essential in a Democracy, that work of that kind, instead of being dishonoured, as it is among us, should be honoured at least as much as, if not above, other occupations.

Harington. That does follow, I clearly see, from your principle, and it brings out the exact point in which I differ from you.

Martin. Yes?

Harington. I mean that what I value above everything else is "virtue," in the pagan, not the christian sense, greatness and nobility of character and mind and body. And I cannot see how, in a world like this, that quality can be acquired and maintained, save by a class living on the labour of others. Manual occupations, trades and commerce, however necessary and

(3) The distribution of labour in a Democracy

respectable they may be, not only do not develop, they tend directly to degrade the body or the soul or both. And this applies to the modern no less than to the ancient world; perhaps it applies even more. We have not, it is true, the status of slavery; but we have division of labour and the machine. And what kind of development is possible, in body or mind, for a man who during six days of eight hours in every week is pulling a lever, or turning a crank, or laying one sheet of paper on another, or arranging type in cases, or any other of the hundreds of thousands of simple and monotonous tasks on which the majority are now condemned to employ the whole of their activity, performing always one single operation which, in itself meaningless and futile, derives significance only from its relation to innumerable other processes, similarly conducted by isolated groups of specialised workmen; so that none of them have any conception of, much less any interest in the thing they are contributing to make, but dismally and blindly grind out their allotted task, unilluminated by the thrill of conception, the passion of creation, the triumph of achievement, not artists, nor even artisans, but in spiritual, if not in legal truth, enslaved, body and soul, no longer, indeed, to human masters but to that most cruel, most implacable, most unnatural monster, the machine. How are such occupations compatible with a noble life? And is it any better when you turn to trade and commerce? Not to speak of the armies of clerks and typewriters, as inevitably degraded in their way as the tenders of machines, what is the real occupation of the masters themselves? Are they not employed perpetually in every kind of mean trick to get the better of one another and of the Public? Are not lying and fraud, under the names of advertisement and competition, the approved weapons of their ignoble war? Is it not their fundamental maxim that "business is business," and does not that mean that business is not loyalty, honour, and good faith? To such men, so employed, how is virtue possible? How is it possible even to professional men, as they rightly are called, for they profess much better than they practise? To plead the cause of justice is a noble act; but to sell a knowledge of law to the highest bidder, without reference to the equity of the case, is the meanest of all forms of barter. To heal the sick is kind and humane; but to pamper rich invalids for a fee, or haggle with the poor for their pence, is to make of the art of medicine a base trade. Wherever and whenever men have, as we say, to "make a living," they make it, the few by fraud and chicanery, the many by servile labour. To no such men is virtue possible. It is possible only—for I will be candid—to those who do not make but take their living; in other words, to a privileged class living on the labour of others, and in exchange, an equitable exchange, as I hold, governing them justly, and fostering those liberal

(3) The distribution of labour in a Democracy

(3) The distribution of labour in a Democracy

arts and sciences in which greatness of personality finds its natural expression. Such a class alone gives a sense and an end to the Sisyphean labour of mankind. And though the many do not directly participate in these nobler activities, yet they are, and dimly feel themselves to be, the happier and better that their sordid and laborious life is redeemed from mere futility by this rare and splendid flower into which it blossoms. But you, by compelling all alike to take part in the drudgery of life, would for ever forbid the plant to bloom; for the sake of justice you would render excellence impossible; all alike would grind in the sordid mill of ignoble toil; and there would be no result, beautiful and good in itself, to contemplate, no product but the daily bread, and no use for that save to enable the workers drearily to renew the daily round. It is because Democracy leads logically to this that I reject it. I must have, at all costs, in any society I could value, colour, splendour, beauty, nobility. I must have it, if need be, at the cost of justice; and unless you can show me a democratic society in which you could guarantee those goods, I deliberately and with a clear conscience choose Aristocracy.

Stuart. May the plain man once more interpose against the passion of the philosopher? Your picture of the spiritual condition of the labouring and professional classes is really a little out of drawing. I don't say that we're saints, or heroes, or philosophers, or poets, but we have our humble virtues and our standards; we are not wholly ignorant, nor exclusively selfish, nor cynically dishonest. We really look, I assure you, better from within than we do from outside.

(3) **The distribution of labour in a Democracy**

Harington. You belong yourself to the most leisured, and therefore the most honourable and cultivated class of business men. Yet it is from you that I have heard some of the most striking illustrations of the mental and moral decadence of the commercial world.

Stuart. Have I so unconsciously given away my own class?

Martin. It is impossible, my dear Stuart, to recognise you as a member of any class. You have none of the characteristic vices. And Harington, no doubt, if you caught him off his guard, would be ready to admit that there may be many men like you. But after all, the general tendency of mechanical labour and of business and professional work is what he describes it, even though individuals may react successfully against it. Moving among men, as you do, with natural kindly feelings, you do not perhaps generally notice the tendency. But stand a little aloof on any kind of ideal standpoint, and Harington's picture, I think, would not seem much overdrawn.

Stuart. I am learning from this conversation that an ideal standpoint is one from which everything is seen out of proportion.

Martin. Well, whether or no Harington's indictment

(3) The distribution of labour in a Democracy

of society as it exists is exaggerated, at any rate I hope to show that things would be better in my Democracy. And everything here seems to turn on this question, whether onerous and necessary labour is, or is not, necessarily degrading to those who perform it.

Harington. I believe it is degrading, both to body and mind. It is the primitive curse; and all the attempts of moralists to convert it into a blessing are sheer sophistry. It is those that look on, not those that work, who talk of the dignity of labour. Is it not, as a matter of experience, the one object of every one to escape from the necessity to work, and especially from the necessity to work with his hands? The whole social organisation, one may say, is a resultant of these two factors, the compulsion to work and the effort to escape from work. The only men who ever lived free and noble lives have been the men who have not had to toil for their living. All the rest are spoilt and maimed by labour.

Martin. Yet, on the other hand, is it not true that many men take to work as a holiday? One turns to carpentering, another to gardening, another to bookbinding, and so on, for the mere pleasure of it.

Harington. That is quite a different thing.

Martin. Yes, but where does the difference come in? The work is the same; what is different is the conditions. The man works when he likes, and as he likes; he works for his own pleasure, not for a tyrannous market; when he is tired he stops, when he is inclined to begin again, he begins. Such work surely, so freely done, is not degrading?

(3) **The distribution of labour in a Democracy**

Harington. No; but you have taken examples where an element of art comes in. And that is not the case with most of the work that has to be done, especially now under machine conditions. Who, for instance, would ever flush drains, or sweep streets, or tend a machine as a holiday?

Martin. I must admit, candidly, that there is a good deal of necessary work which can never be made agreeable or, in itself, desirable. But I believe that the burden of such work might be considerably reduced if men's minds were really set upon that purpose.

Stuart. They are set upon it. What else is the object of mechanical inventions?

Harington. So far as I can observe, their only object is to make money for somebody. I doubt whether anything has ever been invented, or any invention ever been applied, really with a view to lightening toil. Wherever it "pays,"—odious expression!—to employ masses of unskilled labour rather than expensive and elaborate machines, that alternative is adopted. And in the invention and introduction of machines, no care or thought is taken as to the character of the labour which will be required to work them, how exacting, how exhausting, dreary, unwholesome, and so on, but at most, how expensive it will be. So that it could be

(3) The distribution of labour in a Democracy

asserted by John Stuart Mill, and, I believe, with truth, that all our mechanical inventions taken together have not had the effect of lightening the toil imposed upon a single human being.

Stuart. I altogether deny it.

Martin. But perhaps both you and Harington will be ready to admit—and it is important for my case—that if as much ingenuity and patience as has been devoted to the invention of " labour-saving " machines were to be expended upon the problem of really saving labour, it might be possible, by associating with mechanical devices a reorganisation of institutions, not perhaps to abolish but to reduce to comparatively small dimensions the amount of disagreeable and merely onerous work.

Harington. Still, there must remain a considerable residue, and most people must be mechanically and slavishly employed upon it.

Martin. Granted, if you insist upon such hard terms. But, perhaps, in a Democracy, the persons employed need not be of a slavish nature. They might be people of good natural capacity, well-educated, and accustomed to spend a great part of their time in liberal and free occupations. Neither their bodies nor their souls, nor their characters, I think, need be degraded by the performance of the drudgery they undertook; and the utmost extent of their loss would be so many hours of time abstracted from more pleasant and more noble pursuits.

Harington. Those, I admit, would be extenuating circumstances.

(3) **The distribution of labour in a Democracy**

Martin. And then, again, to take the other point you made, as to the chicanery and dishonesty of business and the professions. You were, I think, a little hard upon those pursuits, even as at present organised. But I will not complain of that. I will only urge that here again it is not the occupation that is ignoble, but the conditions under which it is carried on. Suppose, for example, that all those services, or such of them as might still be necessary, instead of being performed, as at present, by private individuals under competitive conditions, struggling for life and death on the inclined plane that leads to ruin, fighting always for more than they need for fear they should be obliged to take less, too many of them, everywhere, competing for one job, and the conditions of success not only, nor even mainly, merit and capacity, still less honesty and rectitude, which may be positive disqualifications, but that peculiar and intrinsically contemptible art we may call "push"—suppose that, instead of all this, all these functions were to be performed by people who received a fixed salary so long as they did their work efficiently —would not all the charges you have brought against these pursuits fall of themselves to the ground; and might not the conduct of those engaged in them become as admirable, and their attitude of mind as independent

(3) The distribution of labour in a Democracy

and as upright, as that of our public servants now in India or in Egypt?

Harington. It might be so, I admit.

Martin. Well, you agree, then, that the antithesis you made between Virtue and Justice is not necessarily final and irremediable? And that Society might conceivably be so organised as to sustain all the burdens of onerous toil, while yet leaving to its citizens leisure and capacity for living noble lives?

Harington. I suppose it is conceivable.

Martin. As conceivable, at least, as your Aristocracy. At any rate, you see the kind of society I contemplate under the name Democracy. It would be one in which the different occupations of men would not be assigned to them fatally, as they are now, for the most part, through hereditary privilege, and as they would be in your Aristocracy by authority; but would be chosen as freely as possible according to the inducements offered, all employments being really, and not only in principle, open to everybody. From which, by itself, it would result that there would be no social classes, though there would be differences of occupation; and from which also, probably, there would result a great mobility of labour, most people being fit for promotion to most posts, and passing in the course of their life through a number of employments.

Stuart. And how do you propose to construct such a society?

Martin. That question brings me on to our next point, perhaps the most difficult and the most important, the distribution of the products of labour. (4) **The distribution of the products of labour in Existing Society**

Stuart. That means the whole question of Socialism and Individualism.

Martin. Yes. Only let us try to set aside all our preconceptions, watchwords, formulæ, technicalities, and look at the matter as freshly as possible, as it presents itself to us in the natural course of our argument.

Stuart. By all means, if we can.

Martin. And shall we, as before, start with our own society, before going on to construct other arrangements?

Stuart. As you will.

Martin. What then is the principle which does actually now determine the distribution of the products of labour?

Stuart. I should say it is the principle of efficiency. Roughly speaking, a man gets what he deserves.

Martin. In what sense "deserves"? Do you mean that he gets what he earns?

Stuart. Yes, approximately.

Martin. But it is clear, in the first place, that a great many people get what they do not earn. For no one earns what he inherits, or what he receives as a gift. (a) **The inheritance of wealth**

Stuart. No doubt; but I wasn't thinking of that.

Martin. Let us, however, think of it first, and note what immense wealth is distributed without any reference to labour or desert. How many millions pass in

(a) The inheritance of wealth

that way every year I do not know; but the sum, of course, is huge. And, as we saw, the existence of classes more or less hereditary, the permanent stratification of society into the rich and the poor, in a word, the plutocratic character of our community, is due to this feature of our system of distribution. We are not, however, now regarding it from the point of view of its consequences, but are seeking for the principle on which it is based. What are we to call this principle? For clearly it is not desert, in the sense that the recipient earns what he receives.

Stuart. Do we require any principle other than the general principle of property? What a man owns he has a right to dispose of, and the man to whom he gives it has a right to receive it.

Martin. A legal right, of course, under our system of law. But it is exactly that system we are questioning and testing. We are asking for the justification of the facts.

Stuart. Well, I suppose you can find it in the fact that a man is responsible for his children. He brings them into the world, and he is bound to provide for them.

Martin. Until, that is, they are able to provide for themselves. Where that responsibility is thrown upon the parents, it is reasonable and right that, when the children are left orphans and are still too young to be able to support themselves, or in case any of them, for one reason or another, should be permanently in need of support, such portion of the parent's property as is required should be devoted to that purpose. But to concede that is surely not to justify the law of inheritance, as it stands, and especially the English law. For we, in this country, do not compel the father to leave any portion of his wealth even to the most tender and incompetent child, but permit him, if he has the mind, to leave millions to strangers, and throw the charge of his children upon the parish. And in no country, so far as I know, is any attempt made to limit the power of bequest to the purpose you suggest. A man, in countries where he is bound to leave some portion of his wealth to his descendants, is bound to leave it to them whether they need it or no, whether they are children or grown men or women, whether they are rich or poor. And while, on the one hand, in the case of the well-to-do minority, it is only incidentally and as it were by accident that the law secures the end which you suggest as its justification; on the other hand, in the case of the great mass of people who have no wealth to bequeath, that end is not attained at all, save by the intervention of public aid or private charity. If really the justification of the institution of bequest and inheritance were that which you allege, it would have to be radically transformed, on the one hand so as to ensure that the purpose in view should be really accomplished, on the other to prevent mere squandering of wealth where it is not needed for the purpose. So long as a

(a) The inheritance of wealth

(a) **The inheritance of wealth**

millionaire can disinherit all his infant children, and bestow his millions on an imbecile or a criminal, unconnected with him by any tie of blood, so long it is impossible to defend the law, as we have it, on the grounds which you advance.

Stuart. Well then, I suppose it can be defended on the ground that unless you allow a man to dispose of his wealth as he likes, he will decline to earn it, and the community will be the poorer.

Martin. There is, no doubt, something in that, though it is hard to say how much. We shall have, later, to examine our system from the point of view of its effect on production. Meantime, and granting your point, we must say, must we not, that in order to encourage the production of wealth our Society permits the distribution of an immense part of it to be governed not by any principle, but by what may indeed be the sound judgment, but may also be, and often is, the caprice and whim of the individual who owns it?

Stuart. I believe it to be more often the sound judgment than the caprice and whim.

Martin. As to that I will not dogmatise. But in either case, it is certain that the law of inheritance and bequest, in the way in which it practically operates, is the great and indeed the only source of our permanent inequalities; and that if we really wanted to get rid of these, should have to modify or abolish that institution.

Stuart. I suppose that is so.

Martin. So much, then, for that part of the distribution of wealth which is determined in that way. We will go on now to another point. A great part of our wealth is in the form, is it not, of rent? I am using the word, you will understand, in the strict economic sense, not in the sense in which it is used in business and in ordinary speech. **(b) Rent**

Stuart. I understand.

Martin. Well then, by definition, rent is something that is not earned by the recipient; it is what he can exact from other people by the ownership of something they need and cannot get elsewhere. Urban ground-rents are the best example; but this element, analysis shows, enters in the most complicated way into the profits of innumerable enterprises; nay, even the professions, even the skilled trades, may be fairly said to include in their remuneration an element of rent, in so far as the price their members can exact for their services is enhanced by an artificial limitation of their numbers, whether that be temporary or permanent. You know, of course, as well as I do, or better, the analysis of the modern Economists.

Stuart. Yes; but I have my doubts of its practical importance.

Martin. In any case, you will not deny the existence of rent, nor the fact that a very large proportion of the wealth of the community is embodied in that form, whether or no it be easy to detect and distinguish from

(b) Rent other elements. And wherever that element occurs there can be no question of desert. Rent is not earned, it is taken.

Stuart. But it is a commodity of exchange like any other, and if a man buys it he has a right to it. If I invest my money in land I have as good a claim to my 3 per cent. as if I invest it in anything else.

Martin. Possibly; but that does not alter the essential character of rent, as wealth not earned by the man who receives it. In a community which made earning the condition of receiving, rent could not be private property, and it would be impossible to buy or to sell it.

Stuart. That, I suppose, may be true.

(c) Interest *Martin.* I believe it to be indisputable. Whatever part of our distribution of wealth may be due to desert, that part is not rent. Let us go on now to another part, the part called interest. On what principle is interest based?

Stuart. Volumes have been written on the subject! And do you expect me to answer in a dozen words?

Martin. I will not trouble you to answer at all, if you agree with me, that whatever may be the justification put forward for interest, it is not earned or deserved, any more than rent or inherited wealth. Interest is something a man can exact because he owns capital; just as he can exact rent because he owns land, or has some other monopoly.

Stuart. Well, if he can exact it, why shouldn't he? He's not bound to lend his money for nothing. **(c) Interest**

Martin. I don't say he is; I am not discussing him, but the institution. In a society where the distribution of wealth was based upon earning, there would be no such thing as interest. For to live upon interest is, so far, to live without labour

Stuart. But the men who administer wealth do labour, and further take great risks.

Martin. That is true of many of them, and on the principle of earnings they are entitled to compensation for that. But such compensation is not interest, it should properly be called wages or salary. Pure interest may best be seen in the dividend, for example, of consols, where the risk is practically nothing, and the recipients need not work at all to earn the income they receive for their stock. Whether or no interest may be justified on some other principle, like that of postponed enjoyment, it certainly cannot be justified on the principle of desert.

Stuart. I don't see that. Economists say, and I agree with them, that interest is the reward of waiting.

Martin. They used to call it " abstinence "; but that grim jest they have been shamed into abandoning.

Stuart. Anyhow, if there were no interest, there would be no saving. And saving is a service as essential to society and as much deserving payment as any other.

Martin. The saving of wealth in order to invest it in

(c) **Interest** industrial enterprises is, no doubt, essential to modern society, and must in some way be provided for. Nor is it easy to see, under our institution of property, how it could be provided for otherwise than by the payment of interest. But under a different institution the same result might be achieved by other means; for the community itself might determine by authority that so much of its annual product should be devoted to that purpose. The service of "waiting" does not seem to me analogous to the service of work, nor to constitute in the same way an equitable claim to reward.

Harington. I am glad to hear you say so; and on that point the common sense of mankind has always been with you. How preposterous, indeed, it must sound to any candid person to say that by not spending a million on immediate enjoyments a man is doing a service that deserves thirty thousand a year for ever! Why, if he wanted to spend his million right off he wouldn't know how to do it! And he would probably prefer to pay a considerable sum not to be compelled to do it! Really, it is time the Economists cleared their minds of cant!

Stuart. One might argue for ever; but the fact remains that society would lose more than it would gain by trying to prohibit interest.

Martin. Possibly! But that only means that interest is a toll we cannot prevent the strong from levying on the weak, not that it is one they are equitably entitled to levy. **(c) Interest**

Stuart. As to equity, there will always be differences of opinion. It is enough for me that interest is necessary.

Martin. Under existing conditions; and, perhaps, under any conditions, in some form or other; but not, I believe, necessarily under the form of a toll paid to private persons, in return for that curious form of service which is called "waiting." However, if any one does put that service on a level with actual work, and assert that a man has an equitable right to be paid for not withholding from other people the means of production, I don't know how I could convince him. I have indicated my position on this matter of interest, and if you do not agree I am content perforce to leave the matter there.

Stuart. I believe I am unreasonable enough not to agree. But no matter! I will not block the way. Proceed with your argument.

(d) Wages

Martin. Well, having ruled out, from the point of view of desert, inheritance and gift and rent and (subject to your dissent) interest, I come at last to the most important factor of all, to wages, under which I include all payments made in return for services performed, whether by the great directors of enterprises, or by professional men, or by manual labourers. You understand that I use the word in the widest possible sense,

(d) **Wages** to include everything that may be said indisputably to be earned. So that here, if anywhere, we ought to find in our Society the distribution of wealth according to desert.

Stuart. Yes; and the greater part of our wealth is so distributed.

Martin. But in what sense are we using the word desert? For I dare say we disagree about that. I should be inclined to say that a man's desert is greater in proportion as his labour, being useful, is also disagreeable and onerous; so that, of two men making contributions to wealth, that one would deserve and should receive more whose work was the hardest to perform.

Stuart. That is a possible view, of course.

Martin. But it is obvious, is it not, that if that view be taken, it is not desert that apportions the rewards of labour? On the contrary, the most onerous and painful and unhealthy work is the worst paid, and the most agreeable, healthy, and interesting the best. So that it is the very opposite of desert, in that sense of the term, that regulates the distribution of wages.

Stuart. Yes; but after all that sense is unusual and strained. In the more ordinary meaning of the term, the criterion of desert does apply. For generally speaking, the man of higher faculties, the man who is more intelligent, more enterprising, better equipped than his fellows, receives a proportionably higher remuneration; and that is just, and as it should be.

Martin. Whether it is just I should be inclined to doubt, unless it be just that " to him that hath shall be given." But whether or no it be just, is it true? Is the bare possession of superior powers enough to ensure to a man a superior wage, and vice versa? **(d) Wages**

Stuart. Broadly, yes.

Martin. I should rather have said, broadly, no. For, as we have seen, in addition to faculty, opportunity is essential to success; and opportunity is distributed without any reference to faculty. The son of a rich man, though he be a fool, may be placed for life in a snug position where he may draw ten times or a thousand times the income of a man of great ability who had the misfortune to be born poor.

Stuart. Such cases are exceptional.

Martin. Are they? That is what I doubt. The exceptions at any rate, I am sure, are very numerous. And even in the cases where it may be true that remuneration is proportionate to faculty, that is not the principle on which wages are distributed, but an accidental consequence of the principle.

Stuart. How do you mean?

Martin. Suppose the number of men of first-class business capacity were to be suddenly multiplied a hundredfold. Would their remuneration continue the same?

Stuart. No.

Martin. Yet it should, if remuneration were measured

(d) Wages by capacity. But clearly it is not, it is measured by supply and demand. Labour, under our system, is a commodity like any other. Its price depends partly on the cost of the production, partly on the demand for it; increase the demand, and without altering the quality of the labour you enhance its price; diminish the demand, and without altering the quality of the labour, you reduce its price. If higher faculty commands a higher wage, that is not because the faculty is higher but because it is rarer. Desert, in any of the senses we have examined, either does not come in at all, or comes in only incidentally. Labour though it were at once the most onerous, the most skilled, and the most productive, might still be paid at the lowest rate, or might even receive no pay at all, if it were in excess of the demand; and similarly, labour the lightest, the most simple, and the least productive might receive the highest remuneration if one could suppose the demand indefinitely to exceed the supply.

Stuart. But the tendency must always be for supply and demand to equate one another. Where services are highly paid, more labour will flow into that line of work, and vice versa.

Martin. That might be so in a perfectly fluid Society; but of course there is no such Society. In fact, unskilled labour cannot flow into the skilled market, nor skilled labour into the professions or into business. Our Society, as we have seen, is an Oligarchy of practically hereditary classes; and these are created and perpetuated by our institution of property. A man's parentage determines whether he shall have access to a crowded or a restricted labour market; and that in turn determines whether his remuneration shall be low or high. The sons of the rich are thus put into a position to continue acquiring riches; the sons of the poor into a position to continue to win a bare subsistence. Make your exceptions as numerous as you like, this is still the rule. There is no principle in the matter at all, there is simply the brute fact.

(d) Wages

Stuart. I think the ambiguous word " desert " has led us upon a false trail. There is a principle in the matter, whether or no you call it desert. A man's reward, roughly speaking, is measured by his contribution to wealth.

Martin. I think it would be hard to show that. What, for instance, is a Barrister's contribution to wealth, and what is a dock-labourer's? Does a barrister add anything? Or does he only subtract?

Stuart. Of course he adds something; business couldn't go on without him. He's there because he's wanted, and he's paid in proportion as his services are valued.

Martin. And his services are wanted, and valued, because men are dishonest, or because the law is doubtful and obscure. Were the community better organised there would be no use for him. He does

(d) **Wages** not produce; at the best he diminishes the friction of production.

Stuart. Well, that comes to the same thing.

Martin. I will not dispute it, as things are. But I will add that, at the worst, when he is engaged, as he often is, in exaggerating not in settling disputes, he is increasing instead of diminishing the friction, and destroying rather than creating wealth.

Stuart. No doubt; but that is not the normal case.

Martin. Well, passing that point, and turning now to the dock-labourer, or to any class of manual workers, they at least are in a very direct, simple and positive sense producing wealth. Now, by what process is it decided that what they produce is worth sixpence an hour, while the barrister's intervention to diminish or perhaps to increase the friction of the industrial machine is worth £10,000 a year? Who makes the calculation and apportions the shares?

Stuart. Those who pay for the services, I suppose.

Martin. But surely they never do. They pay as much as they must, and as little as they can. And the only calculation they make is whether it is worth their while to buy such and such a service at such and such a price. Or do you suggest that if it could be proved statistically that the dock-labourer's contribution to wealth was ten shillings an hour, and the barrister's £100 a year, the remuneration for their respective services would immediately be readjusted to that scale?

Stuart. Not immediately; but it would in the long run. **(d) Wages**

Martin. In the short run, at any rate, you will agree, and the Economists will not deny it, that contribution to wealth is not the measure of wages; and it is the short run in which actual payments are made, and actual equities or inequities developed. Omitting that, however, and taking the long run, even so the intervention of friction of every kind practically destroys the truth of your contention. If, indeed, every one, in all classes, had a perfect knowledge of all the conditions of every labour-market, and if, having that knowledge, they were in a position to bring up their children so as to fit them for any kind of occupation, then it would be true that there would be a constant tendency for wages to be measured by contribution to wealth. But, as it is, nothing of the kind obtains. An unskilled labourer neither knows about the conditions of the better paid kinds of labour, nor is in a position to profit by his knowledge, if he did. Or can you imagine him saying: "I see barristers are paid £5000 a year, whereas I am only getting an uncertain sixpence an hour. I shall therefore make my boy Bill a barrister." The thing is obviously preposterous.

Stuart. You are taking a very extreme case.

Martin. Yes, I am doing so deliberately, to make my point. But the point is a real one. It is only under conditions of absolutely free competition, implying complete mobility and complete knowledge, that it

(d) **Wages** would be true that wages are determined by the measure of contribution to wealth. And such a society, if it existed, would seem to you altogether paradoxical. For in it, it might be manual labour of the lowest kind that would come first and receive the highest reward. There would be a rush upon the more agreeable and interesting work, and away from the dull and laborious drudgery. In consequence, the wages of the latter would rise until they were high enough to attract sufficient numbers of labourers to perform the necessary minimum of work. Low grades of work, if they could not be replaced by machinery, would receive perhaps the highest return, while barristers, doctors, and professors might get a bare livelihood. For, after all, it is the provision of necessaries that must always come first; and in a society of perfectly free competition, those who furnish them would certainly exact a much higher wage than they can obtain under present conditions. And then, it might be found, many people in our class would have to be dispensed with altogether.

Stuart. I suppose that might be so.

Martin. You see then, that while our class-system continues, the tendency, on which economists insist, of every kind of ability to be paid in proportion to its contribution to wealth, is so restricted and hampered that it is, after all, only an ideal indefinitely remote from the fact. The fact, at any moment, is that scarcity determines reward. The more people there are competing for a piece of work, the less they get, and vice versa. And society is so arranged that there are always far more people competing for the more disagreeable and onerous tasks, than for the more interesting and attractive. **(d) Wages**

Stuart. You must, at least, in fairness admit that there are in existence much fewer people capable of undertaking the higher than the lower work. So that the scarcity value is at least a natural and not a social fact.

Martin. Very likely there really is a natural scarcity value of high intelligence. But how great that is we cannot tell until we have perfectly free competition, which involves, among other things, that everyone should have an equal chance of developing whatever faculties he may possess.

Stuart. Well, what do you say is the conclusion of the whole matter?

Martin. I say, summing up my argument, and subject to your correction, that in our existing society the distribution of wealth is determined, to a great extent, without any reference at all to services performed, by the family affections, or it may be the irrational caprices of rich people, bequeathing their fortunes where they choose, and seldom actuated in their bequests by any large view of public policy. And this institution of inheritance and bequest, as we have seen, is the great engine that perpetuates inequalities. It also determines indirectly the distribution of that part

(d) Wages of wealth which passes as remuneration for services. For it maintains the distinction between the rich and the poor; and on that distinction, as we saw, ultimately the apportionment of wages depends, the rich putting their sons into the market where competition is less and remuneration higher, and the poor being compelled to put them into the market where competition is keen and remuneration lower. The distribution of labour and the distribution of the rewards of labour are thus interconnected facts, determined, in the last resort, by our institution of property. And from this institution again results the whole character of our Society.

Harington. Yes; and because this institution has never been rightly ordered, no Society has been rightly ordered. Because of it there always have been, and there still are, at one end of the scale beggars, thieves and outcasts, at the other debauchees, imbeciles and tyrants. Because of it every Society is in a chronic condition of open or latent war. Because of it men's minds and souls are withdrawn from all noble pursuits and concentrated, be they rich or poor, on the mean scramble for wealth or for bread. Because of it all progress is illusory, all culture hollow, all art pessimistic or frivolous, all science sycophantic. Because of it no man's conscience, so long as he retains one, can be at peace. Because of it industry is oppression, leisure extortion, self-culture robbery, and family affection treason. Because of it every occupation is poisoned and every pleasure tainted. Because of it our Society is not a community of civilised men, but a horde of bandits and slaves not knit but aggregated together by the mechanical pressure of fear, cupidity and need. **(d) Wages**

Stuart. Does it really look as bad as all that from the standpoint of the ideal? If so, I'm glad I cannot climb that mountain. What I see, from my own low elevation, is so much more comfortable!

Harington. What do you see?

Stuart. A kind of grey, undistinguished crowd of good-tempered men of business, most of them intent on getting home to the wife, or the garden, or the motor-car; of diligent clerks who cheer the monotony of their daily toil by reflecting on the eminent respectability of their semi-detached villa in the suburbs; of genial, more or less sober, and not too strenuous working-men, full of interest in the King and the House of Lords, in the Pink'un and the 'Varsity match, and generally distrustful of labour-leaders and socialists; of conscientious fathers of families, worried taxpayers, tory publicans, radical peers; the world, in a word, of the nine o'clock train, the motor-bus and the tube. Is that really the same world that you are looking at?

Harington. Yes; but you are looking at the surface, and I at the essential ethical facts.

Stuart. Give me the surface then! on which, after all, most men live. Possibly the victims of our system (as you would call them) ought to be as indignant as you

(d) Wages

are; but I am quite sure that they are not. They're all thinking about their last baby, or their next glass of beer.

Harington. If they are, that makes it worse, not better.

Stuart. Well, I don't believe, anyhow, that they would thank you for your Aristocracy, if you could set it up to-morrow.

Harington. Probably not, nor Martin either for his Democracy. But it is indisputable that either would be much better than what we have got. And you yourself have practically admitted it; for you didn't make much of a defence of the existing order.

(5) The equitable distribution of the products of labour

Stuart. I might have made a better one, perhaps. But, to show how candid I am, I admit that, when all is said and done, I cannot pretend that our system of distribution is equitable. But then I doubt whether one more equitable could be devised.

Martin. May we then go on now, Harington and I, to explain what we think would be equitable, or otherwise desirable, in the communities we are constructing?

Stuart. That, of course, is what I am waiting for.

Martin. Well, we must go very warily here, for we are surrounded on all sides by enemies lying in wait in every bush and thicket, Socialists here, Economists there, ready to pounce out upon us at the least false step, and all knowing the ground so well, and all the paths of error and confusion. What do you say, Harington? Which way are we to try?

(5) **The equitable distribution of the products of labour**

Harington. You must take the lead and I shall follow you as far as I can.

Martin. Can we agree upon this, then, as a fairly safe beginning:—in a well-ordered community no able-bodied person ought to receive anything except as the direct reward of his labour? That seems to me innocent and reasonable.

Harington. I will accept it, subject only to the understanding that in my Aristocracy the work of the governing class is the most important of all; and that they must be well paid for it.

Martin. But how well? Plato, if you follow him, laid it down that his Guardians should have only the bare necessaries of life, on the ground that the possession of wealth would pervert them from their proper function.

Harington. That is where I part company from him. He had in him a strain of asceticism which I cannot approve. He excludes from his ideal polity all art, all magnificence, all beauty, save that which is moral. My object, on the contrary, is to provide on the grandest possible scale for all that aspect of life. Governing is only a secondary function of my Guardians. Primarily they are there to fulfil the ideal of Humanity, not for their own sake only, but for that of the community. They are the representative men; and they must have

(5) **The equitable distribution of the products of labour**

all the resources they require to play that part. They must have great houses, gardens, parks, sculpture, paintings; their dress must be rich and beautiful, their persons magnificent, their retinue superb. They must be like Renaissance princes rather than Platonic philosophers. And for that, of course, they must have great wealth.

Martin. I see. In your polity, then, the claims of the governing class will be unique. There will be no principle common to them and the rest of the community, to regulate the distribution of wealth. They come first and take what they require; and then come the producers.

Harington. Yes; they will be a wealthy class, but a class deserving to be wealthy, because they know how to use wealth for great ends. They will represent for the community the grace, the beauty, the splendour of life, so that their wealth will be a public function, not a private luxury, casting a reflected light upon the masses, who do not directly participate in it, and making them glad and proud to live because there is above them, and in view, a life that is so good in itself. Whereas, in your Democracy, as I see it—and this is my chief objection—though there may be equity, there will be no greatness; and your citizens will suffer dumbly, without knowing why, from the monotonous meanness of their lives.

Martin. You forget that I conceive them to have a

liberal education and ample leisure; and, many of them, to devote their spare time to works of art and imagination. The general interest and delight in life which would be fostered by the conditions I have in view would naturally call for expression on the part of those possessing the gift. Artists and poets and philosophers would not be, as now, people set apart from the main current of life, and obsessed too often by personal, morbid and egotistical emotions; they would be constantly fertilised and refreshed by the stream of common experience, and thus have at once more to express and a keener impulse to express it. Art would be corporate instead of individual; and would find embodiment, not as you propose, in the palaces, galleries and gardens of a wealthy caste, but in public buildings, public parks, public festivals and possessions. It would be the art of ancient Athens rather than of papal Rome; but need it fear the comparison?

(5) The equitable distribution of the products of labour

Harington. Athens was not a Democracy in your sense.

Martin. No; but if it had been, its legacy of beauty and wisdom and power might have been richer, not poorer, than it is.

Harington. Plato and Aristotle did not think so.

Martin. Plato and Aristotle never conceived Democracy as I am conceiving it. And, for that matter, you yourself turn out to be no more a Platonist or an Aristotelian than I am.

(5) The equitable distribution of the products of labour

Harington. I think I might claim to be an Aristotelian, if not a Platonist.

Stuart. Never mind Aristotle and Plato! Modern philosophers are bad enough without dragging in the ancients at every point.

Martin. You hear him, Harington; we must be careful, or he will join the ambushed enemy. Let us get on. I will grant you your point about your governing class; they shall be set aside as an exception. But now, what about the rest of the community? No one, we agreed, was to receive anything except as the reward of his labour.

Harington. Yes.

Martin. It follows then, immediately, does it not, that no one will be allowed to inherit wealth, or to live upon rent, or interest? For these, according to our analysis, are payments made without reference to any return in labour.

Harington. Yes.

Martin. We are led, then, are we not, to the conclusion that the property whence rent and interest accrues must not belong to private persons?

Harington. I suppose so.

Martin. And the fact that inheritance is ruled out leads to the same conclusion. For under that arrangement the property now owned by private persons must revert to the Community.

Harington. We shall be landed then, by this route, in what is called Collectivism.

Stuart. There you are!

(5) The equitable distribution of the products of labour

Martin. There, as you say, we are, or there at least I am for the present. But I am not quite sure about Harington.

Harington. Nor am I. Indeed, it seems clear, when one reflects, that the ownership of property by the Community is incompatible with such an Aristocracy as I am building up. For the ownership of property, under modern conditions, carries with it all other power; and the ownership of property by the Community implies Democracy.

Martin. What do you propose to do then?

Harington. I must vest property, I suppose, in my governing class, who must administer it in trust for the Community.

Martin. They will be, then, much more like Carlyle's "Captains of Industry," or Comte's "Industriels" than like Plato's "Guardians." And the main part of their governing function will be industrial organisation.

Harington. Yes. But of course they will employ trained subordinates. Their own position will be analogous to that of Directors of Companies.

Martin. Whereas, in my Democracy, where there is no governing class, it must be the Community itself that will own land and capital. That is a great distinction between the two polities. They will, however, both have before them the same problem, how to distribute the products of labour among those who are entitled to receive them. So here we are once more back at the danger-point.

(a) Distribution according to need

Harington. Well, start again.

Martin. No able-bodied person, we agreed, is entitled to receive anything except as a reward for labour. But there are always, of course, a number of people who are not able-bodied, children, and the aged, and the sick. And these, we shall probably agree, must receive, so far as possible, according to their needs.

Harington. Yes.

Martin. The question of women also arises at this point. For they, at any rate while they are bearing and rearing children, cannot and ought not to be expected to do any other work.

Harington. No, but the work of child-bearing, so dangerous and painful, deserves reward more than any other.

Martin. I agree. Whatever payments then of that kind may be made should be regarded as rewards for labour, not as concessions to need?

Harington. I should say so.

(b) Distribution according to desert

Martin. Very good. Having marked off then a class of people who are to receive according to their needs, without being asked for any return in labour, we will go on to the more controversial point which concerns the able-bodied. And first, let us take the simplest case and suppose we are dealing with people doing the same kind of work. On what principle shall we apportion wages among them?

Harington. The most reasonable plan, clearly, would be to apportion according to product.

(b) Distribution according to desert

Martin. I don't think that is really so reasonable as it appears at first sight. Because the product depends not only upon the labourer, but upon the raw material, the site, the climate, the machinery and all sorts of other such conditions. For instance, one seam of coal is easier to work than another; one piece of land is more naturally productive than another; one site is more favourable than another, and so on. And there seems no reason why, in a society aiming at equity, some particular set of workers should be credited and debited with these adventitious advantages and disadvantages. To do so would, in fact, be contrary to the principle we began by accepting, for it would in effect be distributing rent to certain privileged labourers.

Harington. I suppose that is true.

Martin. And then, there is another point. Some workers, we must suppose, will be stronger, or more intelligent, or otherwise more efficient than others. Are they to have the benefit of these advantages?

Harington. I suppose it would be only just that they should.

Martin. But would it? That is a fundamental point. For after all, these superiorities are accidental gifts of nature, just as much as soil and climate and site. And why should a man thus fortunately endowed be entitled also to a higher wage?

(b) Distribution according to desert

Harington. There seems to be here a conflict of equities. It seems just, on the one hand, that a man should receive in proportion to his contribution in labour; and, on the other, that adventitious natural advantages should not count in estimating rewards.

Martin. A society would have to choose one or the other principle and it is not very obvious which one is right. But I think it is helpful, in these cases, to ask oneself what would be the course adopted in a society of friends, to which, as far as possible, all societies, in my opinion, ought to approximate. Do you think that, if you and your best friends kept joint household, and made, as you probably would, unequal contributions to the common stock, those who were more efficient would think it right and desirable to claim a proportionately higher share of the joint income?

Harington. No; but I suppose, in such a case, the question might hardly arise. The natural arrangement would be a kind of communism where each took what he most wanted, as indeed is the case in many families.

Martin. It is true, I think, that in a perfect society that would be the rule. But we shall lose Stuart's attention and respect for ever if we suppose such perfection as that. What then, would be the next best course, in a society of friends? Would it not be to measure reward not by product but by effort, so that

(b) Distribution according to desert

anyone, though he were weaker or stupider than the others, if he were working equally hard, would be entitled to an equal share? In that way one would discourage deliberate idleness.

Harington. That seems to me, certainly, a more friendly arrangement than the other.

Martin. And would it be less just?

Harington. No, I do not think it would.

Martin. And I think it would be more just. Shall we then accept that principle, and see what follows?

Harington. I am content.

Martin. It follows then, does it not, that a weaker or stupider man, working harder than one who is stronger and more intelligent, but producing less, ought to receive a higher wage?

Harington. Yes.

Martin. And I think, further, that on the same principle it would follow that the kinds of work that are more disagreeable and tedious and exhausting, ought to be paid proportionately higher. For the principle on which we are proceeding is, that rewards should be proportionate not to output, nor to faculty, but to painful effort incurred?

Harington. Yes.

Martin. But hark! do you not hear the arrows of all the Economists in ambush whistling about our heads? What are we to do? Shall we ignore them, and go on, only admitting, in case it should appease them, that

(b) Distribution according to desert

this principle, like any other, would be difficult to apply in detail, and might be subject to many exceptions and uncertainties; but insisting that, if adopted, it would certainly lead to quite different results from any other; so that it really is a guiding principle, which it is very significant and important to lay down?

Harington. I am quite ready to go on. I'm not afraid of the economists.

Martin. Perhaps you do not know as well as I how formidable they are. For my own part I never like to have them against me. However, we must do our best to get on and dodge them, if we can. We were speaking, were we not, of the distribution of rewards among people working at the same or similar tasks; and if we are to apply our principle here, where the character of the work, agreeable or the reverse, is the same for all, we shall have to say that they ought to be paid in proportion to the amount not of their product, but of their efforts.

Stuart. And how are you going to determine that?

Martin. There you see! That was one of the Economists' arrows. What are we going to do about it?

Harington. Pull it out, and come on!

Martin. There's only one way of pulling it out, and that is by making a concession. I do agree that, in the same job, it would be difficult, in any detail, to apportion wages to effort. Some general system of wages, time or piece, there would have to be; and to

(b) Distribution according to desert

make numerous exceptions to it would be too complicated to be practicable, though provision might and should be made roughly to secure that no one was penalised by age or sex. On the whole, however, I am ready in this matter to sacrifice to expediency what our principle asserts to be justice, to pay according to a general scale, and let the workers secure the rental value of their natural advantages.

Harington. Do as you like.

Martin. But then I intend to be all the stiffer about the application of our principle to the next case, that of workers in quite different occupations. It will give us results that sound very paradoxical; but I mean to adhere to them bravely, however much we are assailed.

Harington. What is it that is so paradoxical?

Martin. Remember what we said before, that, as things are now, all the occupations that are most interesting, stimulating and delightful, that employ the highest faculties, and are the most worth doing for their own sake, are, broadly speaking, the best paid, while those that are sordid, dreary, mechanical, dehumanising, hardly receive a living wage. Is not this a fact which the Economists themselves must admit if they are candid? I hope they hear what I am saying behind the trees!

Harington. I, at any rate, do not dispute it.

Martin. Well, but in a society regulated by our principle, is it not clear that exactly the opposite will be the

(b) Distribution according to desert

case? That it is the sordid, dreary, physically and morally exhausting work that will be the highest paid, and the nobler and more delightful kinds the lowest?

Harington. Certainly that follows, and it seems to me to be just.

Martin. We shall have then a scale of wages running the opposite way to the present scale; and perhaps bankers like Stuart will be getting sixpence an hour, and dock-labourers £5000 a year.

Stuart. You had better duck as quick as possible, or you'll have a fine whizz of arrows about your ears!

Martin. I've ducked, but I stick to my proposition. I shout it in the ears of the enemy! Come on, Stuart! What have you got to say?

Stuart. Oh, nothing of importance! Only to point out that, under such a scale, you will get no one to do the higher kinds of work at all!

Martin. Should I not? But why not? If you had to choose between being the director of a business at a low wage, or a flusher of sewers at a high one, would not you be likely to choose the former? Of course, as things are, you demand £5000 a year, because you can get it! But if you couldn't get it? Or couldn't get it except by doing some work you loathed? Clear your mind of the preconceptions you have derived from existing conditions, and my scale will not seem to you so absurd.

Stuart. But it's clear anyhow, if I am to take you

(b) Distribution according to desert

seriously for a moment, that the higher kinds of work require for their efficiency a higher salary.

Martin. I assume that my community will not be so stupid as to offer a wage below the level of efficiency. In that respect it will be more intelligent, I trust, than the society in which we live. For, as things are, many of the higher kinds of work are paid much more than is required for their efficiency, and many of the lower much less.

Stuart. You admit then that your principle would have to be modified by this other principle of efficiency?

Martin. Certainly. I am not assuming a society of unpractical pedants, but one that will aim at as much equity as is found to be compatible with efficiency. The mere fact, however, that it may be necessary to qualify one's principles does not make it any less important to lay them down. Have you any other objection?

Stuart. I have one which includes all others—that I can't imagine how such a system would work; or how, or by whom, such a scale of wages could be devised and enforced.

Martin. That is, of course, a real difficulty; and when we come to deal with it, we may find we have to modify our principle of equity. Meantime, however, I wanted to lay down what the principle seems to me to be, reserving the question of how it might be carried out. On the principle itself have you anything else to say?

(6) The relation of the productivity of Existing Society to its system of property

Stuart. Of course I have! I have everything! I don't know where to begin, or end! But take this point, which is absolutely fundamental. Under your system, as I understand, rent and interest being ruled out, and inheritance forbidden, it will be impossible for any one to accumulate a fortune; and those who have most will be broadly those who do the least skilled and most laborious work.

Martin. Yes.

Stuart. Very well, then what becomes of the stimulus to production? The world is kept progressing, from the economic point of view, by the chance given to able men of making great fortunes. Take away that motive, and everything flags. And what is the use then of all your elaborate system of distribution, when there is practically nothing left to distribute?

Martin. Nothing?

Stuart. Well, nothing to speak of. Are you aware that, at this moment, if you divided equally the income of this country, there would only be about £40 a head?

Martin. I have heard something of the kind.

Stuart. Well then, don't you see that the problem of distribution is really negligible, compared with that of production? And if your reformed society is going to check production, its scheme of distribution will be worse than useless.

Martin. No one who believes, as both Harington and I do, in a society which is based upon material well-

(6) The relation of the productivity of Existing Society to its system of property

being, will deny the importance of maintaining production. But that, surely, is a technical, rather than a social problem, and lies outside our range of inquiry.

Stuart. Not at all; it is a social problem. I maintain that the particular system of property which now prevails is peculiarly favourable to production; and that the system you suggest would be peculiarly unfavourable.

Martin. Well, let us see if that is really so. Your contention, as I understand, is that the main stimulus to production is profit, and that no man will put forth all his powers unless he sees a chance of making a fortune.

Stuart. Yes, broadly that is true.

Martin. And would you also assert that no man will put forth his powers if he can get all he wants by doing nothing?

Stuart. Yes.

Martin. In that case, our system of property, in so far as it gives people incomes without requiring any return in labour is, on your own showing, unfavourable to production; and inheritance, and interest, and rent are as unjustifiable from this point of view as from that of distribution.

Stuart. Not at all; Every one knows that inheritance is a great stimulus to production, because people continue to work and save for the sake of their families,

(6) The relation of the productivity of Existing Society to its system of property

even when they have earned all they want for themselves.

Martin. Even if that were as true and as important as is generally assumed, you must still set against it the fact that the heirs of great wealth are, so far, on your own contention, directly discouraged from production. I don't know, and I don't see how anyone could calculate, which of these factors counts for most; but I submit that it is at least not obvious that the power to bequeath wealth is more of a stimulus to production than the reverse.

Stuart. There is no doubt whatever about it.

Martin. Is that so? How do you strike the balance? I will however admit that our system encourages energy; only, let us see more precisely how. And first, the source of the energy is, is it not, in your view, simply the passion of cupidity?

Stuart. Yes.

Martin. And this cupidity works, first, in a more passive form, among all the people who have any sum great or small, to invest; and then, more intensely and actively, among those who make it their business to create and foster enterprises, that is, financiers and capitalists.

Stuart. Well?

Martin. Well, these men, clearly, whatever else they are, are not the originators of ideas. It is not they who are the discoverers and inventors, but quite a different kind of man, the sort of person they despise as academic and unpractical, actuated by a passion which also they would despise, if they could comprehend it, the love of truth. Dalton and Faraday, Clark Maxwell and Kelvin, these men were not financiers, nor capitalists, nor were they moved by cupidity; yet it is upon them and their like, more than upon anything else, that the progress of production depends.

(6) The relation of the productivity of Existing Society to its system of property

Stuart. Granted, in the last resort. But it is the capitalists who supply the stimulus and the means and the intelligence to apply discoveries and inventions successfully to the practical arts.

Harington. That they may take all the profits themselves and squeeze out the inventor! The function of the financier, backed by the dividend-hunting public, is to exploit the man of genius, and deprive him of his reward.

Stuart. You can put it so if you like; but I insist that it is a socially useful and indeed indispensable function.

Martin. But one that might perhaps be otherwise performed and in a way more profitable to the community.

Stuart. That is what I deny.

Martin. But consider; the one motive of the exploiter being to make money for himself and incidentally for his shareholders, he and they will always be ready to make it at all cost to society. It will not matter to them whether what they produce is a good thing or a

(6) The relation of the productivity of Existing Society to its system of property

bad thing, so long as it is one for which, by fair means or foul, they can create a demand. They are as likely to devote their energies to poisoning the community as to feeding it, if the community, as is unfortunately apt to be the case, responds to the invitation to be poisoned.

Stuart. The root of that evil is that people have perverted desires, not that other people give them the means to gratify them.

Martin. My point is that, under this system of production, prompted by the cupidity of irresponsible people, bad desires just as much as good ones are evoked and converted into effective demands. For it must always be remembered that supply determines demand at least as much as demand supply; and that intelligent men armed with capital may alter indefinitely the taste and morals of a nation. One sees it constantly whenever the West comes into contact with the East. The immediate effect is the disappearance of all taste and beauty in the arts, and the substitution of inferior western for superior native goods by the joint operation of greed at the one end and cheapness at the other.

Stuart. The capitalist is only giving scope to desires that are already there waiting for satisfaction.

Martin. Or say that he plays on the instrument the tune he prefers, and that his tune is apt to be very low and vulgar. Nay, when he comes to deal with uncivilised peoples, what he plays is a dance of death;

for he does quite deliberately, and with a clear conscience, exterminate them by cheap gin unless the public authority intervenes. I will not however labour this point; but I will ask you to bear it in mind as part of the case. And also to bear in mind this: it is no part of the capitalist's aim to husband the resources of any community. If he can pay big dividends, say for fifty years, that is all he need trouble about. The future of a country or a society is nothing to him, for he will not be there to make money out of it. So that, for instance, he will always be in a feverish haste to exploit natural wealth at all and every cost to the community. He will cut down its forests, exhaust its mines, spoil its climate, and ruin its population body and soul—as was done in this country and in all countries during the industrial revolution until the State stepped in to stop it, and as is being done before our eyes at this moment in the Congo Free State, not to speak of cases nearer home. All this he will do without ruth, without shame, without reflexion even, if, in his short-sighted book-keeping, it seems to pay him to do it.

(6) The relation of the productivity of Existing Society to its system of property

Stuart. You make him a kind of monster!

Martin. Not at all! I credit him with being a good father of a family, a church-goer, a giver to charities, a sportsman, a member of Parliament. He's no worse than you or me or any shareholder. But the system of providing in this particular way the stimulus to and the direction of production does lead to these consequences,

(6) The relation of the productivity of Existing Society to its system of property

and they must be set off against its undoubted efficacy as a developer of energy and intelligence.

Stuart. I think you exaggerate enormously.

Martin. My dear Stuart, it is your constant cry! Perhaps I do, perhaps I do not; there is no scale to weigh the truth upon. It is enough for me to have reminded you of what you cannot honestly deny, that our method of flinging upon the resources and the populations of the world the unconscionable greed of capital, is open to these very grave objections. I might add others, and especially those which are recognised as the " wastes of competition," advertisement, over-production, adulteration, commissions and all the rest of it. But I have said enough to remind you that the price paid for our method of stimulating production is a pretty heavy one.

Stuart. Of course there is a debit side to the account.

Martin. Yes, and not a small one; and we have not yet completed our summary of it. For if now we turn from entrepreneurs and capitalists and investors and their operations to the great mass of working people, here too what waste do we find!

Stuart. Where, exactly?

Martin. Well, to begin with we have always with us a large number of paupers; and they, of course, are not productive.

Stuart. They are, for the most part, aged and sick people, who in any case would not produce.

Martin. But also there is a large class of permanent loafers and tramps.

(6) The relation of the productivity of Existing Society to its system of property

Stuart. Yes.

Martin. And a great number of people who are unemployed, at least for some portion of the year.

Stuart. Yes, and it is very regrettable; but these are not results of the institution of property.

Martin. Not directly, perhaps, but indirectly. Bad houses, bad education, lack of opportunity and pressure of need, in other words, poverty, are responsible, at least as much as original sin, for the creation of the class of the unemployable. And poverty is the other side of riches, and both are aspects of property. And as to the temporarily unemployed, they too are the victims of a system which gives to private persons, working for their own profit, the control of the natural resources of the earth and of the accumulated products of labour, while divorcing them from all public responsibility for their trust. No economic fact can be dissociated from the institution of property; and if you are to claim for it what you regard as its advantages, you must permit me to point out its drawbacks.

Stuart. I am permitting you.

Martin. The existence, then, in our society of large numbers who need not, of others who will not, and others who cannot work, must be set off against its claim to stimulate production.

(6) The relation of the productivity of Existing Society to its system of property

Stuart. Still these, after all, and in fairness, are exceptions.

Martin. Very well; let us turn then to what may be said to be the normal fact, the great body of active workers in full employment. The bulk of these are, no doubt, kept continually at work, not however, by the chance of a great fortune, but by the constant and unremitting pressure of need. They live from hand to mouth, and from day to day, and to cease from labour is to face starvation. Certainly, then, they are compelled to work under our system of property, just as is the ass who turns the wheel at the well. But if we ask whether their work is as productive as it might be under other conditions, the answer, I think, must be very doubtful.

Stuart. Why so?

Martin. Well, to begin with, none of them have been properly educated; so that they are not in a position to make the best use of such powers as they possess. And how much wealth is lost to the community by this simple fact, by lack of intelligence and initiative among working men, it would be impossible to estimate.

Stuart. Well, we have public elementary schools to educate them.

Martin. No doubt; to that extent we have violated the principle of our system of property, and admitted a socialistic leaven. But even so, as things are at present, the kind of education given in these schools does not compensate for the drawbacks of a poor home. Poverty must be held responsible for an indefinite loss in productive power. But, further, putting that aside, the bulk of wage-earners have not really sufficient prospect of advancement to stimulate them to put out their full powers. They are compelled to work; but they are not tempted to work their best. It is true, no doubt, even in Europe, that a man can rise from bottom to top of the social scale. But the difficulties are so immense, the talent and character required so great, the opportunities so few, that in effect the stimulus is only felt by a negligible minority. Broadly speaking, the wage-earners are members of closed castes; where they begin, there substantially they will end; the wages they were earning as young men they will be earning still, likely enough, in middle life; while their old age, in all probability, will be spent in the workhouse. Under our system, then, they are indeed under compulsion to labour, and so far the system encourages production; but they have no spur to labour otherwise than mechanically and reluctantly, no prick of ambition, no light of hope, no beckoning and expanding future. And how incalculable must be the loss of productivity there!

(6) The relation of the productivity of Existing Society to its system of property

Stuart. There is some loss, no doubt.

Martin. I will not wrangle with you how much. But when all that I have said is taken into consideration, how much really remains of your claim for our system

(6) The relation of the productivity of Existing Society to its system of property

that it is peculiarly favourable to production? This much, I think: that the few who get a good education and a good start in life, and who are not paralysed by a competence or ruined by a fortune, are in a position to make their own way by their wits. It is these who feel the stimulus of the great prizes, these who are impelled to certain forms of material production by a combination of opportunity, need and ambition unattainable perhaps under any other system; these who become our great organisers and financiers and captains of labour. And on these our attention is so exclusively fixed that we take them as types and symbols of our whole society, forgetting that they are a very small minority, and that the bulk of men have neither their chances nor their motive to make the most of them.

Stuart. They may be a minority, but they are a minority of the utmost importance. Upon them depends all progress in material prosperity.

Martin. I will not dispute it; and any society, no doubt, would be the poorer which could not evoke the full extent of their capacities. Possibly, however, that result might be achieved in the better-ordered societies we are imagining.

Stuart. I don't see how.

Martin. Well, Harington at any rate can say, I suppose, that he has only to breed a class of inventors and organisers, and give them their appropriate work and the problem is solved. In his society, in fact, the

(6) The relation of the productivity of Existing Society to its system of property

money wage would apparently not be required as a motive, but only as a means of providing adequate resources for each class of workers. Wouldn't that be so?

Harington. Yes, I think it would.

Stuart. No doubt! Harington has begged all the questions! But then he can't expect one to take him seriously.

Martin. Does that imply that you take me seriously?

Stuart. Not very, I confess. Still, you don't seem quite so much in the air.

Martin. Thank you. And in return I will not at this point lay too much stress on my system of breeding for a high average. But I will ask you to remember that in my society, in which there are no distinctions of class, whatever advantages there may be of education and opportunity will be distributed fairly to all according to their different choices and talents. And I may assume, accordingly, a higher level of intelligence, a higher average standard of life, and a more general sense of scope and outlook than exists at present among the mass of workers. That is really not very chimerical.

Stuart. Well?

Martin. Well, then it follows, I should say, that you will get such a development of intelligence and energy applied to every branch of work as we at present can hardly conceive. For masses of people who now mechanically grind out their work, uninspired by hope

(6) The relation of the productivity of Existing Society to its system of property

or interest, will begin to think about it, to reflect upon its problems, to want to master and improve processes, and generally to become human beings with human aspirations, instead of living tools.

Stuart. Why should all that happen?

Martin. Because not only will they be better trained and equipped, but the sense of injustice and of inferiority, of being merely "hands," will have disappeared. They will be, and feel themselves, responsible citizens of a community, in as good a position as anyone else, receiving substantially just treatment on a system known, approved, and maintained by themselves. The civic feeling which, among the masses, is non-existent now, and hardly could exist in a community so chaotic and unjust as ours, will germinate and grow into its full proportions. And if you add to this that, being educated and intelligent people, they will want to employ their faculties for the mere pleasure of doing so, and will naturally be glad, many of them, to employ them in the occupation they have chosen, I think you ought to agree that any loss there might be from the disappearance of the opportunity to make immense fortunes might be more than compensated by the operation of these other motives and forces.

Stuart. Possibly.

Martin. And let me go further into what you will call idealism, but what I am inclined to think is common sense. Able men, I believe, do not really care about money to the extent you seem to suppose. They value money as a test of success. But suppose it ceased to be the test? Suppose all the standards changed, as they must do, by direct consequence, if such institutions as I am imagining were introduced? What, then, would stimulate your able man, the sort of man who now makes his millions? Why not the recognition his fellow citizens would give him for his services, a recognition which might take the form of honours and titles, but would be best expressed in a general respect for his person and deference to his judgment? Come, my dear Stuart, are men, even now, really so sordid as you and most of the Economists make out? Or are we not all, rather, involved in some hideous and transitory nightmare, which obscures and travesties to us our own nature?

(6) The relation of the productivity of Existing Society to its system of property

Stuart. I can't say anything about that. I take men as I find them.

Martin. Well, I will not try to allure you into utopian admissions. But, after all that I have said, will you not, at least, admit that it is not so obvious as you assumed, that such a society as I am trying to build up need come to grief for lack of productive energy?

Stuart. Perhaps it is not obvious. But I still think it likely.

§ 5. Government

Martin. Well, I must leave the matter there, and go on to the next point. We have laid down generally what we hold to be the equitable system of distribution;

Government and we have endeavoured to meet the objection that a society adopting such a system must be less productive than our own. But we have yet to face the difficult question, which you raised some time ago, as to how such a system could be maintained.

Stuart. Yes! How is your society going to be governed, or to govern itself?

(1) Is government necessary?

Martin. There is a question we ought logically to ask first. Is it necessary that it should be governed at all?

Stuart. What do you mean? Of course it must be governed.

Martin. But what is government? Is it, after all, what really moves a society? Or is not every society moved by its habits and needs and desires, resulting in that we may call its will?

Stuart. But government, I suppose, is the ultimate expression of that will.

Martin. Clearly it is not its complete expression; for though it limits, it does not prescribe most of the activities of men in any civilised society. Even among ourselves, complicated and elaborate as our law has become, it is voluntary contract and voluntary association that determine most of the relations of life. People buy and sell, hire and engage, combine in every kind of way, for purposes of business or amusement or instruction, in thousands of complicated ways, determined by their needs and desires; and though the general forms of such action, and the general limitations upon it, are prescribed by law, under penalties, yet the particular content in every case is created by the individuals contracting and combining, who even overleap, in pursuit of their aims, national boundaries, and form an intricate network of social and economic relations with people living under different laws and different government.

(1) Is government necessary?

Stuart. That, of course, is true.

Martin. It follows that, on the face of it, we need not conceive government to be essential to a society. We have to consider whether it is or no, before asking what form it should assume.

Stuart. The question is, surely, rather academic. No one doubts that government is essential.

Martin. Anarchists not only doubt, but deny it.

Stuart. But we are not, I hope, going to take our counsel from them.

Martin. We shall take our counsel, I hope, as hitherto, from our argument. But I want to examine, not to take for granted, the expediency of government. And first let us ask in what way the rules made by government are distinguished from those which people make for themselves in all these forms of voluntary association of which we have just spoken.

Stuart. They are distinguished, clearly, precisely by the fact that they are not voluntary. People find them made for them and have to submit to them under penalties.

(1) Is government necessary?

Martin. Coercion then, I suppose we may say, is the essence of government. And if that coercion be really necessary it is because there are people in the society who want to break the rules and will do so unless they are deterred by fear.

Stuart. Of course; there is the criminal class.

Martin. Yes; but why? If people want to break the rules, it must be because they judge them not to be advantageous to them. And if they are not advantageous, must they not be, in some way, wrong?

Stuart. Excuse me, but is it worth while to go into all this? It must be as clear to you as it is to me that it is not the rules but the people that are wrong.

Martin. I am sorry to seem tedious, but it is just because that is not clear to me that I am raising the point. For I see no reason to assume that the rules made by government, either now or in any former time, really further in all respects, or even in most respects, the true interests of the community. I do not mean merely that the community may not know its true interests, though that of course is quite likely to be the case; but, putting that aside, there seems no reason to assume, but on the contrary good reason to deny, that governments have ever aimed at the interest of the community.

Stuart. I am not a historian; but that seems to me on the face of it an extraordinary statement.

Martin. The more you studied history the more I

believe you would be driven to think that, extraordinary though the statement may seem, it represents the fact. For all governments hitherto, as we had occasion to remark before, have been government by and for some class of the community, and have kept in view in the first place the interest of that class. To maintain themselves in the position of rulers and property-holders, and to keep others in the position of labouring for them, has been their first, if not their only object. And this is as true of governments called Monarchies and Democracies as of those which are recognised as Oligarchies. The best of monarchs, a Frederick the Great, or a Joseph II., intended in all their legislation to perpetuate the distinction between those who work and obey and those who appropriate and rule; and the famous democracies of the ancient world were based on slavery. There has never been a government hitherto which has intended the Good of all, in the sense of intending for everyone equal opportunity and an equitable wage.

(1) Is government necessary?

Stuart. Well, putting aside history, of which you have more knowledge than I, do you maintain that in our own time no government intends the Good of the community?

Martin. Not if our earlier analysis were right, that existing societies are Plutocracies tempered by Ochlocracy; for governments support the institutions which produce and perpetuate that form of society. Or do

(1) Is government necessary?

you see any government which intends seriously to alter them?

Stuart. I see in all governments much more tendency to Socialism than I like.

Martin. I do not deny—it is in fact my hope—that for the first time in the history of the world a movement may be on foot to convert society into a true Democracy. But meantime governments, as always, reflect the form of the society. They exist primarily to support plutocratic institutions; and are therefore, like all that have preceded them, governments by and for a class, the class of the well-to-do. And if that be so, the coercion they exercise is not likely, in all or in most respects, to be exercised for the Good of the whole; nor are those who resist it likely to be merely criminals, in the sense of people incapable of and hostile to right social relations. If, for instance, as to a great extent is admittedly the case, crime springs from poverty and ill-education and neglect and lack of opportunity, it springs from the very institutions which it threatens, and government indirectly creates the criminals it punishes. And not only so, it also creates them directly, by the penal system, as many competent and experienced people have long been insisting. This coercion, then, so far, is really a bad thing, deserving the reprobation of the anarchist. And we have still to see whether there is any coercion that would be good.

A POLITICAL DIALOGUE

Stuart. Do you suggest the immediate destruction of government by way of reforming Society? (1) **Is government necessary?**

Martin. I do not; but only because human nature, I believe, is so intricately entangled in its institutions that it could not in a moment adapt itself to better ones. That, however, is a point for future discussion. At present, what I want to suggest is this, that if government, in the sense of coercion, has hitherto been essential to society, that is because no society has yet been founded on equity. The laws have been made by one class for another; and there was no reason, other than fear, why that other class should obey them. But when we come to imagine an ideal society, would government, in this sense, be essential to it?

Stuart. I suppose there would always be recalcitrant people.

Martin. Why should there be? What makes people recalcitrant, save the fact that they are expected to obey rules of which they do not approve?

Stuart. But make your institutions as just as you like, and your people as public-spirited as you like, there must always be differences of opinion as to this or that law or regulation; and if those differences become acute there must be a point at which coercion comes in. For example, even in your ideal Democracy, a controversy might arise over religious education such as that which has lately been distracting the country.

Martin. I hope that in my ideal Democracy there

(1) Is government necessary?

will be more tolerance and common sense. Still, I agree that it would be hazardous to anticipate, even under better institutions, an immediate disappearance of the necessity for coercion. But on the other hand we may fairly say that the more equitable laws and institutions can be made, the more they will be respected; that the knowledge that they are constructed with a view to nothing but the public Good would make minorities more patient and more law-abiding; and that, as Society perfects itself, at once in men and in institutions, the element of coercion will become less and less important until it imperceptibly disappears. So that really the contention of the Anarchists that a just society would require no government, in that sense of the word, is substantially true.

Harington. But Anarchists, as I understand them, go further than that. They seem to object not only to coercion, but to regulation.

Martin. It is not easy to see whether they imagine regulation to be unnecessary, or suppose that it will always somehow arise spontaneously from the mind of the mass. I conceive the latter to be their idea; and I think myself that it is fanciful. If men are to co-operate in immense numbers, over immense areas, in an immense number of matters intricately connected, as is the case in the societies we are imagining, as well as in that which exists, they must, as now, be subject to very complex rules; these must be fixed over periods of time; there must be a recognised machinery for framing and modifying them; and they must interfere with the momentary moods, caprices, and desires of individuals. The kind of freedom Anarchists seem to desire, in which no one is ever obliged to do anything he doesn't at the moment want to do, is ruled out no less by the natural than by the social conditions of labour. Nature fixes the season and time for many kinds of work, without any respect to our moods; and co-operation requires a readiness on the part of the co-operators to fulfil fixed obligations at fixed times. But, with these exceptions, the Anarchists are right in desiring to leave to the individual as much liberty as possible, and to involve him as little as may be in hard and fast rules. And that brings us back to the question, what will be the functions and the form of government in our ideal societies, taking government now in its sense not of coercion—for we suppose, on the whole, a willing obedience—but of regulation. And, to take the functions first, these will clearly be very different from those which have to be performed by existing States.

(1) Is government necessary?

Stuart. Yes; and they will also be, so far as I can see, far more vexatious. Every detail of everybody's life will be regulated; and the fact that you use the word regulation instead of the word coercion will not make the interference any the less intolerable.

Martin. I am not so clear about that. But we shall

(1) Is government necessary?

be able to judge better when we have brought before our minds the full extent of the interference of existing governments.

(2) The extent of governmental interference in Existing Society

Stuart. Existing governments, of course, are coming to interfere more and more, and I think it very regrettable. But, after all, what do they do? In brief, they protect us from disorder at home and from aggression abroad.

Martin. Yes; but let us see what is involved in that. Protection from disorder at home means punishing those who break the law; but the law, as we have seen, means poverty, as institutions now are. So that the maintenance of order means the maintenance of economic unfreedom for the great mass of citizens; and indirectly, if not directly, government is responsible for all the limitations of personal development which we saw to be characteristic of modern societies.

Stuart. That seems to me, if you will pardon my saying so, a little sophistical. I was speaking of administrative interference; and it seems clear that there must be much more of that in the communities you call ideal than in our own society.

Martin. Possibly; but the evil of interference consists only in its restriction of liberty. So that I am surely justified in suggesting that we lose, perhaps, under existing conditions, as much through economic unfreedom as we gain through administrative independence. If, in the communities we are imagining, everyone had the best possible opportunity to develop all the resources of his nature, submission to regulations devised with that purpose would surely be a small price to pay.

(2) The extent of governmental interference in Existing Society

Stuart. It is a question of temperament, I suppose; but I should think it a very heavy price.

Martin. You and I, you must remember, belong to the small section of society that has both kinds of freedom; and I think it possible that we really have, on the balance, more liberty than we could easily secure under other conditions; though to my mind, the value of the liberty is almost destroyed by the knowledge of the price which others have to pay for it. For those others, the mass of men, what freedom really have they? Can they effectively choose their career, more than under the most bureaucratic socialism? Can they fix their hours of work? Can they determine their wage? Can they travel? Can they educate themselves? Can they select their society? Can they assure their solitude? They are at least as absolutely under the regulation of their masters as they could be under that of the community in a completely socialised State; and they have not the compensating advantage of security, of comfort, of leisure, which it is reasonable to think might be guaranteed to them under the institutions we have been imagining.

Stuart. Well, I still call it paradoxical to attribute that kind of unfreedom to the interference of government.

(2) The extent of governmental interference in Existing Society

Martin. Let us turn then to another great branch of governmental activity. In national defence, at any rate, you will not suggest that government does not interfere with its subjects? In this country, it is true, it contents itself with taking our money from our pocket, £60,000,000 yearly, to pay for a mercenary fleet and army. But abroad, every citizen, for one or more years of his life, is torn from his home and his occupation, shut up in barracks, and subjugated without appeal to the despotic orders of public officials; while later he is liable, for the greater part of his life, at any moment to be called away from his work, his habits and his family and set marching to shoot or be shot by people against whom he has no grievance in a quarrel which he doesn't understand. Can any interference with individual liberty be imagined greater than that?

Stuart. And your ideal community? Is it to have no enemies and no war?

Martin. I dare not digress into that immense subject, for our hands are already overfull. I will ask you therefore to make a great concession; and since we are considering the internal order of a community, to abstract from international relations, that we may concentrate on the other point. I admit of course that this course is unscientific, and even unphilosophic; but if we try to treat of everything at once, we shall never be done.

Stuart. It wasn't I, it was you, who introduced the subject.

(2) The extent of governmental interference in Existing Society

Martin. I agree, and it was an error. I will withdraw that part of my indictment against our society, if you will withdraw your challenge to mine.

Stuart. Be it so.

Martin. Neglecting then, in the communities we are imagining, the question of war, what remains for us to discuss under the function of government?

Stuart. There remains, of course, what we spoke of at first, the regulation of industry. And that is where the socialistic tyranny comes in.

Martin. Yes, and also where the individualistic tyranny goes out.

Stuart. What do you mean by that?

Martin. I used the word tyranny because you used it; but we will adhere, if you prefer it, to the more neutral word regulation. And clearly such regulation, which I called individualistic, now exists, through and through, in every branch and in every detail of industry. Wages are regulated; hours of work are regulated; methods are regulated; prices are regulated; only all this is done by private persons or companies, instead of by government officials. So that it is not, I suppose, regulation to which you object, but some particular method of regulation?

Stuart. I object to regulation by outside officials who don't understand business.

(2) The extent of governmental interference in Existing Society

Martin. Naturally. And we shall have to see whether we cannot imagine, for our ideal community, some method not open to that objection. Let us try then to sketch such a method in outline; for it would obviously be silly and pedantic to elaborate details. What we have to aim at, I suppose, is as much elasticity and as much efficiency as is possible in a very extensive and complicated machine. And here I see a great distinction between the possibilities of Harington's Aristocracy and my Democracy.

Harington. What is that?

(3) Government in an Aristocracy

Martin. How would you propose to organise industry in your community?

Harington. My organisation, I conceive, would be quite frankly what is called paternal. From the industrial point of view my governing class would resemble Carlyle's "captains of industry."

Martin. Or rather, they would resemble the Saint-Simonian aristocracy. For they would combine, so far as I see, the spiritual and the temporal functions to a degree never known before; inasmuch as they would be responsible at once for culture and for industry, and all ownership would be vested in them. So that their power and responsibility would be far greater even than that of Plato's Guardians, and, also, of course would be extended over a far greater area.

Harington. That is so. But remember that we are postulating Plato's device of scientific breeding; and also, I will add, an appropriate system of education for all classes. (3) **Government in an Aristocracy**

Martin. We must hope then that the breeding and education of your governing class will make them equal to their duties. But, however, so far as our present point is concerned, what we have to notice is that liberty can be no feature of the aristocratic state.

Harington. That depends on what is meant by liberty. At any rate, what I propose does not involve any coercion felt as oppressive. For everyone would be assigned exactly the function for which he was fitted by nature, so that he would be doing exactly what he would choose to do, if he could choose freely; and being unoppressed by any sense of restraint, of faculties thwarted that might have been developed, all my citizens, it may fairly be said, will be free in a sense which applies to almost nobody under existing conditions.

Martin. But that sense is, is it not, the sense in which a stone is free when it falls? Your citizens will have been so narrowly specialised at their birth, and so exactly furnished with the appropriate tools and conditions, that no question of self-determination can ever arise. To call them free would be, I think, paradoxical; but I gladly admit that they would not be slaves. They would realise, all of them, all the possibilities with which they were endowed at birth; they would therefore be contented and orderly; and the task of govern-

(3) Government in an Aristocracy

ing them, however difficult from its complexity, at least would not be magnified by the insubordination of the subjects. But such a community clearly is not what is commonly understood by a free community; rather it would naturally be described as an immense bureaucracy.

Harington. You may describe it as you will, so long as we understand that it would be orderly and beautiful, in the Platonic sense; and also, in his sense, just.

(4) Government in a Democracy

Martin. It is not yet time to characterise it, until the description is completed. We will call it then, with your permission, a Bureaucracy; and it will, I think, be tedious and unprofitable to say any more about its system of government. Everything would be regulated by the governing class, or by officials appointed by them; and the problem of combining popular control with efficiency, and liberty with order would not arise. But with my Democracy it is far otherwise. For there is no governing class; the Society must govern itself; and it must preserve the utmost liberty compatible with the necessary regulation. And that is a very difficult matter to arrange.

Stuart. I should think it is! You have committed yourself to Collectivism; and that means that you have to regulate everything. And the more perfectly you can do that, the more completely you must abolish liberty!

Martin. How terrifying you are when you assume

the cap and gown of the schoolmaster! I feel like a small boy who has made a mistake in prosody.

(4) Government in a Democracy

Stuart. You've made a mistake in something much more serious than prosody.

Martin. But please, sir, may I explain?

Stuart. Excuse yourself if you can! If not—!

Martin. The cane is waiting, I know! Well, I must do my best to escape. I have to show, if I can, how my citizens can be regulated without being converted into slaves. And first, please remember that it is they who are to regulate themselves.

Stuart. That's a mere phrase. Regulations, even if they be adopted by a majority, are none the less felt as restrictions even upon the members of the majority.

Martin. Still, I may fairly assume, I suppose, that whatever rules are adopted will be supported by public opinion? Whereas you, perhaps, like many critics, are unconsciously supposing that the arrangements of a collectivist community would be imposed upon members as recalcitrant as yourself by a kind of mysterious junto called the Government.

Stuart. Any government always is, and always must be, out of touch with public opinion.

Martin. Please, sir, is that a law of nature?

Stuart. It's a law of experience!

Martin. And down comes the cane! But, seriously, it is, is it not, preposterous to assume anything of the kind? At any rate, I can only continue my argument,

(4) Government in a Democracy if you will admit that the rules a society obeys may be such as it does effectively approve.

Stuart. Oh, if you appeal to my clemency! Pray go on.

Martin. I have, then, only to consider what kind of rules a free society would be likely to tolerate and to impose upon itself.

Stuart. If you go upon those lines you will find that no free society would ever tolerate Collectivism at all.

Martin. That's what I want to examine. And, first, let us remind ourselves what are the principal matters such a society might wish to regulate. There was, to begin with, marriage.

(a) The regulation of marriage *Stuart.* The most intimate and private of all matters! Are you going to determine by authority who is to marry whom, and how many children they are to have, and all the rest of it?

Martin. I confess that I can hardly imagine any free community submitting in that matter to direct coercion. It is conceivable, I think, that they might be persuaded, or rather persuade themselves, to forbid under severe penalties the marriage, or at least the production of children, by people known to be suffering from hereditary diseases. That would at any rate be something.

Stuart. Is that as far as you would go?

Martin. It is as far as I like to suggest going by way of coercion. But I hope much from inducement and much from public opinion.

Stuart. What do you mean by inducement?

(a) The regulation of marriage

Martin. I mean attracting people to the right course, rather than deterring them from the wrong; a most important principle and one which has not been nearly enough employed by governments.

Stuart. How would it apply in this case?

Martin. You may remember that, in discussing the rewards of labour, we agreed—at least Harrington and I did—that the work of bearing and rearing children was as necessary and important as any other and ought to be paid for as such.

Stuart. I remember something of the kind was said.

Martin. Well, that arrangement, if adopted, might be used to favour the right kind of marriages. For the payment might, and indeed obviously should, only be made to those parents whose union is approved by the society. So that, though there would be no coercion, save in the case I mentioned, to prevent people marrying as they chose, there would be a special preference given to such unions as were likely to result in better children.

Stuart. But that would involve some system of public inspection.

Martin. No doubt! If you were to receive the payment, you would have to be passed as fit for marriage.

Stuart. That would be very much resented.

Martin. If it were, it would remain inoperative. But I do not agree with you. I believe that public opinion

(a) **The regulation of marriage** is ripening more and more to the importance of this point; and that it is as much ignorance as indifference or unwillingness, even now, among better educated people, which maintains the present haphazard arrangements. I admit, however, that, in this matter, more important than any regulation is the progress of knowledge and education and sound opinion. Given such progress, I believe the kind of regulation I suggest might be found both workable and effective.

Stuart. Well, I hope I shan't live to see it!

Martin. I hardly think you will. You may fairly expect to enjoy, during the rest of your life, the satisfaction of knowing that, in the interest of liberty, hundreds and thousands of children are yearly born into the world slaves to disease and every kind of misery. In my democratic state, on the contrary, it would be the parents who would be made what you call slaves in the interest of the liberty of the children.

Stuart. Oh, I won't use the word "slave." We aren't fighting a general election. Besides, I admit that, on this point, your propositions are more reasonable than I expected.

Martin. Thank you! May I go on then?

Stuart. Do.

(b) **Education** *Martin.* The next matter to deal with should perhaps properly be education. The constructors of Utopias have usually given a large place to it, and rightly. Nevertheless, I want to be excused. The subject is too big to treat incidentally, and we have our hands more than full.

(b) Education

Stuart. I'm very glad to escape from that subject. I hate it!

Martin. I will only say, then, that I assume a system of free education, open to all alike in all its grades, though not all would be compelled to pass through it. That, in principle, I think offers no particular difficulty, and is likely to be realised even in communities not based on Collectivism.

Stuart. Yes, I will not quarrel with you about that.

(c) The regulation of industry by authority

Martin. We come, then, at last, to the great crux. What about the regulation of industry?

Stuart. Precisely! and that's where you come to grief.

Martin. Here at least, you mean, I am bound to set up an intolerable tyranny?

Stuart. Yes.

Martin. And I, on the contrary, insist that, even if I were obliged to have recourse, in the regulation of industry, to sheer authority—exercised of course through laws approved by the community upon the individuals who have approved them—that even then a collectivist society might fairly claim that in all important essentials it was freer than our own.

Stuart. What!

Martin. I do really think so! because, you see, I maintain that, for most people, no real freedom exists as things now are.

(c) The regulation of industry by authority

Stuart. How can you maintain that for a moment in the face of the facts?

Martin. Well, let us look at the facts, clearing our minds from cant! What do we see? Where is the freedom? Is not everybody who is working at all dependent upon the work of everybody else; must he not adjust to them his hours, his movements, his place of residence, suffer from their negligence or misfortunes, fail with their failures, or succeed with their success? How many business or professional men, to take only the freest classes, can decide on any particular day:—"I don't feel like work. It's a fine spring morning. I shall sit in the garden, or take a ride," or whatever it be that inclination may dictate. You know very well that they are driven like slaves (as you would say, if they were under government orders) to take the early train, to go to the City or the Courts, to toil all day in a close, unhealthy, noisy atmosphere, to return home fagged and dispirited to a late dinner, and afterwards, at the best, to fall asleep, at the worst to sit up into the small hours of the night preparing for the next day's work. "What a life! What a life!" you would cry, if a socialist government were to impose it upon them.

Stuart. Because it would really be a much worse life in that case. I admit your point; I admit that in our own society almost no one is free, in the sense that he can dispose of his time as he likes. But at any rate we aren't under orders. We chose our profession in the

(c) The regulation of industry by authority

beginning freely, and thereby chose, once for all, all its disabilities. And if we sacrifice to it all or most of our leisure and our liberty, we make that sacrifice freely, day after day, because we deliberately decide that it's worth while. It is our own judgment, our own prevision, which we obey, not somebody else's. And the difference is infinite.

Martin. You are not under orders, you say; and I admit it. But who are you? How many are there of you in that happy position? Need I once more labour the point that almost everybody is an employee of somebody else, under the strictest orders every day and all day, bound to fixed hours of work, to a fixed routine, in all weathers, in any state of health, under the strongest of all sanctions, the threat of starvation? And as to the free choice of occupation, have we not sufficiently illustrated how limited in practice that is for the great mass of people; and indeed, for large numbers, non-existent?

Stuart. No matter, for I am going to be stiff about this; and I insist that even an ordinary unskilled labourer benefits by, and consciously enjoys, his freedom under the present régime. As a matter of fact, however dependent his position may seem to be, he takes his risks and has his chances. He gets drunk and doesn't go to work for a couple of days. He takes a holiday off without asking. He has a row with the foreman, and gets the sack. The threat of starvation

(c) **The regulation of industry by authority**

does not in fact paralyse his action. If he leaves his job he may always get another elsewhere, or always thinks he may. If not, he goes on the tramp, he falls back on charity, he commits a crime and goes to prison. At every point, however narrow his limits, he does, within them, move at his own choice. And that I hold to be a priceless privilege, even for the poorest and weakest, and one which ought not to be bartered for the richest mess of pottage.

Martin. If you put it so, even a collectivist community could not take away that measure of freedom. If a man prefers to take the chance of starvation or prison, rather than perform his allotted work, no one can prevent him in any kind of society, other than one of literal slave-driving by the chain and the whip, which, I suppose, even you will not imagine Collectivists to contemplate. It would, I admit, be very disturbing to the Democracy which I have sketched if any considerable number of people adopted those tactics. But if they did, they must, so far as I can see, be free to do so. By doing so long enough and in sufficient numbers, they could break the society; but the society could not break them. The very most it could do would be what we now do, give them the choice of work or starvation or prison. So that that particular liberty, which I do not admire as much as you do, would persist, though I do not think it would be taken advantage of, even in a collectivist community.

(c) **The regulation of industry by authority**

Stuart. You score a dialectical point; but I am not convinced. There would, I am sure, be less freedom, in a very real sense, under Collectivism than there is now, not only for the few but for the many. Take only one point. Everybody would be told by public authority not only what occupation they were to pursue, but where they were to pursue it. They could not even change their house without leave, even within the limits of the same district.

Martin. Terrible indeed! But, after all, need we doubt that it would be found both possible and convenient to transfer people from one place to another, just as now postmen or railwaymen are transferred, often enough at their own instance and to suit their own desire, so far as that is compatible with the exigencies of the service? The freedom to change one's abode is very limited, as it is, for most people; it might be more limited under Collectivism, or it might not; it is impossible to say. But, anyhow, the difference would be a comparatively small one of degree.

Stuart. I don't think so. And then there's another point. There could not really, in your Democracy, be any freedom of supply and demand. The community would decide what was to be made, and in what quantities, according to an elaborate calculation as to the average demand to be anticipated. I don't discuss now the practicability of that—to me it seems altogether chimerical; but supposing it to be practicable,

(c) The regulation of industry by authority

I say it would be intolerable. All the desires of minorities, all taste and caprice, would be sacrificed to the steady mass-demand of necessaries. No one would be allowed to make, and no one therefore able to obtain, the thousand expensive luxuries that soon become cheap necessaries, the innumerable things that presuppose and keep in existence a love of beauty. In effect, whether intending it or no, your collectivist state would end by enforcing a Spartan regimen. There would be no variety, no change, therefore no progress; nothing but what, in your favourite "Republic," one of the characters calls a life of pigs.

Martin. It would indeed be a terrible state of things if everybody were provided with necessaries, good food and houses and clothes, space and air and health, and nobody with champagne and motor cars and fruit out of season. A life of pigs, indeed, in comparison with that large, humane and civilised existence now enjoyed by the poor in Whitechapel, and the rich in Park Lane.

Stuart. You may be as ironical as you like, but I am not moved. What I am saying now is what I believe, however badly I may say it. I think your regulated life would be intolerable. But also I think—for you shall hear it all—it would prove impossible. You have always stopped me when I have begun to express my doubts; but now I'm not going to be muzzled any longer. Your Collectivism strikes at the root of the only motive force capable of holding society together at

(c) The regulation of industry by authority

all, and keeping it at once in equilibrium and in movement. You despise self-interest; but it would be as reasonable to despise the law of gravitation. The whole social universe is governed and sustained by it. What possible order, laid down in rules and supported by officials, could approximate to the marvellous efficiency of this unconscious co-operation? Try to realise it! Every want provided for as fast as it finds effective expression, capital saved in exact proportion to the demand for it, talent and ability and labour of every kind flowing exactly to the place where it is wanted because it receives exactly the reward necessary to attract it, a general balance of supply and demand more minute, more complicated, more extensive, than the intelligence can comprehend with all its efforts. Yet all this taking place of its own accord, by the simple fact that everybody is always acting freely (I repeat the word) under the stimulus of self-interest. This thing is really happening; it actually exists. And you quietly propose, in the name of some impossible perfection, to weaken indefinitely, if not altogether to suppress, this immense and all-pervading energy, to abolish the liberty in which alone it can find play, and to substitute for this harmonious and spontaneous adjustment the clumsy and bleared-eyed rules of an army of mediocre officials, supported by the chimera of a universal public spirit. I say that even if men were all little Catos and Hampdens they could not, with the

(c) The regulation of industry by authority

best will in the world, create a single wheel or gear of the astonishing mechanism, or achieve a hundredth part of the beneficent effects that result automatically from the independent efforts of individuals under the system which we actually enjoy.

Martin. What idealists we all are! Even you cannot escape.

Stuart. What do you mean?

Martin. I was only reflecting how naturally and unconsciously you substitute for the actual facts what one may call the economic scheme; the general account of tendencies which, no doubt, are really operative but which never at any moment realise that to which they tend. All that you have said, as you well know, must be qualified by that discouraging phrase "in the long run." And it is in the short run that all the inequities, cruelties, and maladjustments happen; for it is the short run that comprises and includes the whole life of individual men. Besides, you have omitted to take account of friction. You have described the model of the machine, how it would work if it worked perfectly with perfect materials. But, in fact, it works roughly, with very coarse stuff. It jerks and jams and sticks, it breaks threads, it tears material; and every shock, every rupture, every retardation or acceleration operates in the substance of human lives. The groans and screams of that engine, as it jars on its ruthless course, come from the tortured lips of men and women.

Stuart. And do you suggest that there would be no friction in your community?

(c) The regulation of industry by authority

Martin. No! What I was maintaining was, that in a collectivist society, even though it were worked entirely by authority, there might really, for the mass of the people, be more freedom, not less, than there is under our present system. For they would have better education and opportunities, and they would not be more tied and bound in their industrial life than they now are.

Stuart. You can say what you like, but such a society would be intolerable. I infinitely prefer our own conditions with all that is unsatisfactory about them. And so, I believe, would all men, at any rate all Anglo-Saxons, once the alternatives were fairly before them.

(d) The regulation of industry by inducement

Martin. You are very uncompromising; but I am glad to think that it is not, after all, my scheme to which you are so radically opposed.

Stuart. How do you mean, not your scheme?

Martin. I do not propose, myself, that everybody's occupation shall be assigned to him by authority.

Stuart. How are you going to work your society then?

Martin. Very much as our own is worked, by attraction and repulsion. For the real characteristic of existing society is not its freedom but its automatism. And this automatism I propose to retain, so far as it is compatible with the principles of my democracy.

Stuart. What do you mean by automatism?

(d) The regulation of industry by inducement

Martin. I mean that, though people are not for the most part free to choose any career they like, yet, within the limits imposed, they do choose; their occupation is not imposed upon them by law. Again, though they cannot really make effective demands even, in many cases, for necessaries, still less for superfluities, yet such demands as they can make effective do get supplied, without any direct intervention of government. And that kind of machinery is, in itself, a better kind, I should agree, than public regulation, supposing it could be made equally efficient in securing a desirable result.

Stuart. I am glad, at least, that you admit that.

Martin. Certainly I do; for, in the first place, it is difficult for officials to adjust their rules to the real trend of demand; and, in the second place, rules, as such, are disliked by the better kind of man as well as by the worse. I propose, therefore, to maintain the existing automatic system, so far as it can be made to contribute to my ideal.

Stuart. But can it?

Martin. Let us see. And let us take first this important point, the choice of an occupation. What do you say is the present system?

Stuart. That everyone chooses, within the limits of his powers and opportunities, the occupation that seems to him to present the greatest advantages; with the result that there is a constant adjustment of demand to supply, people crowding into those occupations where they are most wanted because there the inducements offered are the highest, and vice versa.

(d) The regulation of industry by inducement

Martin. Subject, of course, to all the exceptions and qualifications I have dwelt upon. Well, in my community, I am going to have exactly the same machinery, only much better adapted to its purpose. I am going to attract people where they are most wanted by offering them higher wages, or other differential advantages, and vice versa. Only, as my competitors will really start equal, so far as social advantages are concerned, I shall get a much better adjustment of occupations to demand, and to individual taste and talent, than is the case now.

Stuart. How will you do all that?

Martin. By a scale of wages and hours of work fixed by officials, whose business it will be to deal with that matter. Thus, for instance, when they find there is too little labour offering itself, say, for agriculture, and too much for the cotton industry, they will put the wages up in the one, and down in the other until the supply equals the demand.

Stuart. But if you fix wages as they are fixed now, by a scale of supply and demand, what becomes of your other scale of equity?

Martin. Just there is the beauty of my system! For the tendency in my society will be, contrary to the tendency in our own, for the two scales to coincide.

(d) The regulation of industry by inducement

Stuart. Why?

Martin. Because of the equality of opportunity. Consider for a moment! If you had a society composed of really equal units, and you set before them a number of different tasks, some attractive, some the reverse, and had to get all these tasks fulfilled by the method not of coercion but of inducement, you would have clearly to weight the more disagreeable work with advantages just sufficient to overcome the comparative reluctance to engage upon them. The advantages might be higher wages, or shorter hours, or anything that would serve the purpose. But the point at which they were sufficient to evoke the necessary response would also be the point of equity, according to my scale. For the extra disagreeableness of the work would be exactly compensated, in the worker's own judgment, by the extra reward.

Stuart. That is ingenious enough. But in your society, though you postulate equality of opportunity, you can hardly pretend that your units will be really equal.

Martin. No, not exactly; and that of course does away with the exactitude of the equity. If you weight an employment with advantages enough to attract all the labour you want, some of your labourers, no doubt, will be getting more than they strictly should. But the principle is sound; and we must be content to put up with some lack of precision in its application.

(d) The regulation of industry by inducement

Stuart. And then there is another point. I presume that in your society some kinds of ability will be rare. And on the method of remuneration which you now propose, it will be open to those possessing the ability to hold up their services for a high price, as they do now. So that natural ability will be able to receive a reward which according to your analysis is really rent.

Martin. That is true. But I shall be willing to make that concession for the sake of ensuring the easy working of my society. And, after all, as we admitted at the time, it is one view of equity that a person is entitled to all he can secure by the superiority of his natural abilities. I don't think my Democracy need take any great exception to that, supposing it were otherwise convenient.

Stuart. Still, it does involve abandoning your professed principle of equity.

Martin. I said at the time that I might have to modify it when we came to deal with this point. But I don't consider the objection very important. For under a system of true equality of opportunity it would be found, I expect, that particular kinds of ability are less rare than they appear under our conditions, where so much talent never gets a chance of development. I think that, substantially and in the main, the supply-and-demand scale and the scale of equity would tend to coincide, and that the deviations need not seriously trouble us.

(d) The regulation of industry by inducement

Stuart. They would, perhaps, trouble you more seriously than you suppose. But I have made my point, and I need not dwell upon it.

Martin. Well then, to pass to the next matter, the other great crux of my Democracy will be the adjustment of supply to demand in commodities. And there too I propose to preserve the principle of automatism.

Stuart. How?

Martin. The authorities will raise the price of goods, other things remaining equal, as the demand increases, and vice versa. This would be a signal, as it is now, for an increased production of those commodities of which the price was rising, and therefore, of course, for an increased application of capital to the processes of producing them.

Stuart. The saving of capital, and its application, would be a great difficulty. As things are, it is accomplished automatically by the operation of the rate of interest. But in your community there will be no interest and no private savings. The community, through its officials, will have to decide how much capital shall be saved and to what it shall be devoted.

Martin. That is true; and in making the calculation the officials must be guided by the conditions of demand, actual or prospective, as private capitalists are now. The only difference is that the motive will be not private greed, but the public advantage; and that there will be no appropriation of interest by individuals.

Stuart. Your officials, and your community generally, on whom they depend, will have to be very intelligent and very far-sighted!

(d) The regulation of industry by inducement

Martin. My institutions will tend to make them so. But will you admit that by such arrangements as this a collectivist community might realise the minimum of regulation and the maximum of automatism?

Stuart. The automatism would only be partial. The scale of wages and the scale of prices would determine the choice of occupations and the character of production, as now. But these scales themselves would be fixed by authority.

Martin. Yes.

Stuart. But conceive the difficulties! You would have to provide, in the first place, officials at least as intelligent and capable as our best business-men now are.

Martin. I shouldn't despair of that. I believe that we in England habitually over-estimate the ability of business-men, and under-estimate that of officials.

Stuart. I don't agree with you. But, even so, business-men, you must allow, have a motive to make the best of their ability incomparably stronger than any that can influence officials. For their whole success or failure in life, their fortune or their ruin, depends upon the results of their efforts.

Martin. Their motive is meaner, but it is not necessarily stronger. Even as things are, I think that the achievements of our civil service, at home and abroad,

(d) The regulation of industry by inducement

show that the motive of the public good, and of an honest man's self-respect, is sufficiently strong to serve the purpose.

Stuart. Granting it were—for one can argue for ever inconclusively enough about such matters—there is still another difficulty even more formidable. The government of your society, of course, will be democratic?

Martin. Yes.

Stuart. That means, then, that the officials will be more or less directly controlled by the people whose wages they fix, the prices of whose goods they determine, and a portion of whose produce they are setting apart to form capital, instead of permitting its employment in immediate gratification. Well, just imagine the complications! Every branch of labourers will be trying to keep up their own wages, and to depress those of other branches; and all the labourers together will be trying to spend as much as they can on themselves, and to set aside as little as possible for future generations. At present, when people save, they save for their own children; but the community as a whole have not, for the descendants of the community as a whole, the feeling a father has for his own offspring. How then, under these conditions, can you expect your system to work? Granted that the officials were as capable and as public-spirited as you choose to suppose, —which in itself is an immense and unwarrantable assumption,—yet a Democracy would never allow them to operate in the true interests of the community. Every trade would be against every other trade; and all together would be against the interests of the future and in favour of those of the present generation.

(d) The regulation of industry by inducement

Martin. I wish I were less candid than I am! How easily I should answer you.

Stuart. How could you answer me?

Martin. I should overwhelm you with check and counter-check, with local and central councils, with inspectors and commissioners and committees, with competitive examinations, and security of tenure, and all the machinery of government. I should admit frankly that every individual, and every trade and occupation, would always be trying to cheat the community; and then I should claim to checkmate them all by the ingenuity of my institutions. But I can't do it! Candour compels me to admit that a community whose morals should be such as you describe, would make very little except confusion and disaster of any form of Collectivism.

Stuart. Well, there's my case!

Martin. A very formidable one! But let me, though I have abandoned one obvious line of defence, try at any rate to make something of another. Let me put in some considerations why the public morals of a collectivist community might be higher than you suppose.

(d) The regulation of industry by inducement

Stuart. Of course, have your say.

Martin. My main point is that such a community would be the first one in the history of the world whose institutions were founded as nearly as possible upon equity. Every citizen could inspect them, and they would have nothing to fear from his inspection. Again, for the first time in the history of the world, government would have as it object the interests of the whole community, and not that of a governing class. We are also supposing that our citizens are intelligent and well-educated. All of them would understand the reason of their public policy, and would see it to be a policy for the public Good. If then, as a necessary incident in that policy, this or that interest should temporarily suffer and this or that other temporarily gain, I should expect not stupid and blind resistance, but convinced and intelligent acquiescence. Nor do I imagine the citizens of such a community to be so short-sighted about their own interest as to refuse to put aside from their income of to-day what is necessary to provide the capital for their income of to-morrow. The necessity for this is so clear, so irrefutable, so simply demonstrable, that I consider it preposterous to suppose that it would not be recognised. Nor, again, do I conceive them so indifferent to their descendants as to be unwilling to make provision for them. It is true that they would, I think, rightly, decline to make unnecessary sacrifices. They would probably, as we have already suggested, limit their families. They would not undertake all the burdens of the future and leave to their descendants all the benefits. But they would presumably care for their children, as people do now; and if the care were largely collective, where now it is individual, I do not agree with you that it need therefore be less efficient. It would require no great effort of intelligence to understand that the welfare of one's children was bound up with certain sacrifices of immediate enjoyment demanded by the community. And, that once understood, it is taking no very utopian view of human nature to suppose that the sacrifice would be willingly made. In brief, my case is that you infer too readily from the attitude of most men now towards a government whose activities they but partially identify with the public interest, to their attitude towards a government really of their own creation, and existing simply and solely to administer institutions based upon a generally recognised equity. The one thing is as different as possible from the other; and it is not a foolish idealism to maintain that in a collectivist community the problem of government might solve itself far more easily than the opponents of such a society are willing to admit.

(d) The regulation of industry by inducement

Stuart. It might, but I do not believe it would.

(e) Unregulated Industry in a Democracy

Martin. And I cannot prove that it would, any more than you can disprove it. Only experiment can decide. But since you would not be willing to experiment in

(e) Unregulated Industry in a Democracy

my direction, shall we try whether we can compromise? It might be possible to preserve as much automatism as we have in our own society, and yet to secure as much equity as I demand for mine.

Stuart. How would you propose to do that?

Martin. I propose that you should do it.

Stuart. I! What have I to do with it? I'm the critic, not the constructor.

Martin. Still, you maintain, pretty consistently, a point of view. You are the champion of what you conceive to be liberty. And my suggestion is that, having worked out the plan of a Society, or rather of two societies, upon the basis of justice and equity, we now turn to your basis, and see what kind of results it will give us, if we build upon it consistently. Perhaps it may be a result we can both accept.

Stuart. Nothing is less likely, I should say. However, try by all means.

Martin. It is you who ought to take the lead here, for it is your thesis we are to develop.

Stuart. No, I decline altogether. I'm here under protest and upon sufferance, to try to keep you and Harington sane. It's not my business to build. I don't profess to be an architect.

Martin. I must do my best then, subject to your correction. You say, as I understand, that liberty ought to be the basis of society.

Stuart. Yes.

(d) Unregulated Industry in a Democracy

Martin. But what do you mean by liberty?

Stuart. I mean something quite precise—freedom from governmental regulation.

Martin. You are an Anarchist, then?

Stuart. Do I look like one?

Martin. Not at all, I confess. You look like a man who believes in property and the police.

Stuart. You do me no more than justice!

Martin. In that case we shall have to discover for your principle something more precise than freedom from governmental regulation. For no regulation is more constant, more crushing, more radical and severe, than that which is involved in property and the police. In consequence of them a kind of man survives and comes to the top who might otherwise either not exist, or occupy the most degraded position. Just imagine, to illustrate my point, the sudden dissolution of government, so that our rich men and captains of industry could no longer call upon the public force to protect their persons and property. What a transformation scene it would be! I seem to see Mr. Carnegie and Mr. Pierpont Morgan and Lord Rothschild and other great men on the run, puffy, exhausted, mad with terror, having suddenly discovered that they have no personal force or capacity to secure anything that they have got, let alone acquiring any more; I seem to see professors, like myself, impotent and dazed, asking charity of sturdy ruffians; I seem to see the financiers, the

(e) Unregulated Industry in a Democracy

lawyers, the men on the stock-exchange, at their wits' end, while all the good things of the world are being divided up among those who, for the moment, are morally or physically ablest to get hold of them and to keep them.

Stuart. Those wouldn't necessarily be the poorest people.

Martin. Certainly not. Some of the younger bloods on the Stock-Exchange, who keep up their athletics, would have quite a good chance, though I'm afraid the great financiers and bankers would come off badly. But however that might be, after a very short period, in which order, wealth and culture would disappear, there would ensue a state of permanent insecurity, in which, at any moment, the physically strongest, most cunning, and so on, would assert themselves as the most powerful. Such, I suppose in your view would be a state of complete freedom from governmental regulation. And since you do not approve of that, I must ask what it is you do approve and desire to bring about.

Stuart. I want, of course, the greatest amount of freedom from governmental restraint that is compatible with the system of private property.

Martin. But what is the principle, or ideal, that makes you value so highly private property, that you are willing, in order to secure it, to admit this great engine of government?

Stuart. Isn't all this rather elementary and superfluous? Of course, like all sensible men, I value private property as the necessary condition of that free activity of individuals which leads to the greatest sum of material wealth, and so of progress.

(e) Unregulated Industry in a Democracy

Martin. All individuals? Or some privileged ones?

Stuart. No, all.

Martin. I may take it then, to begin with, that you, like me, are a Democrat, and that, so far, you side with me as against Harington.

Stuart. Yes, I think I do.

Martin. Some kind of equity, then, you admit, as well as some kind of liberty?

Stuart. Of course!

Martin. If then, it could be managed, without any sacrifice of liberty, that in each generation everybody at birth should start equal, so far as external advantages are concerned, and that all should then be free to develop their faculties, you would have got something like the system you seem to desire?

Stuart. Yes, I think so.

Martin. Your principle then is really that of equality of opportunity?

Stuart. But only so far as that is compatible with liberty.

Martin. It is, I think, compatible with liberty, in your sense of the term; only, if we work it out, it will give us, I think, a society almost as different from our own as Harington's Aristocracy or my Democracy.

(e) Unregulated Industry in a Democracy

Stuart. How so?

Martin. That is what we must see. And first, to get clearer about liberty. You said that you meant by it freedom from governmental interference as complete as may be compatible with private property, and, I suppose I may add, with security of person, and the obligation of contract.

Stuart. Yes.

Martin. But by private property what are we going to mean? Are we to mean necessarily all the incidents and forms it now assumes in the law of western states?

Stuart. That is what I meant.

Martin. I must raise the question, then, whether you ought to mean it; whether, that is, you could not better arrive at your professed ideal, which is to combine freedom from public regulation with equality of opportunity,—whether you could not arrive at that by some quite different system which would still admit of private property? I suppose you are willing to discuss that question?

Stuart. Certainly.

Martin. Well, then, I must remind you, to begin with, that, under our present system, there is hardly even an approximation to equality of opportunity. That results clearly from all our previous analysis. Opportunity varies with classes, and classes are numerous and exclusive. Some open the gate to an idle life, others to the professions, others to clerical work, others to skilled trades, others to unskilled labour, others to starvation. Generally speaking, we admitted, did we not, that that was so.

(e) Unregulated Industry in a Democracy

Stuart. Subject to the fact that there are opportunities to pass from one class to another.

Martin. Yes. But still the broad fact is as I described it. And why? Partly, no doubt, because the children of those who monopolise any grade of work have specially favourable opportunities of being introduced to that work. But, primarily, because we permit the private inheritance of wealth. Now it seems clear that to abrogate that part of the law of private property would not at all diminish liberty, while it would, or might, indefinitely increase equality of opportunity.

Stuart. But there comes the difficulty. If property is not inherited by individuals, it must revert to the community. And then, either at once or by a gradual process, according as you make your transition, you fall into Collectivism, which is exactly what we are proposing now to avoid.

Martin. Let me distinguish! We fall, I admit, into the public ownership of land and capital; but not necessarily into its public management, which is what I understand by Collectivism. And just here comes in the difference between the Democracy I worked out and the society we are now constructing. We must admit public ownership; we need not admit public management.

(e) Unregulated Industry in a Democracy

Stuart. How would you arrange that?

Martin. In a way that is already familiar enough in practice; as, for instance, whenever a Public Authority owns the tramway-system and leases it to a company. Why should not that plan be indefinitely extended? Why should not the Public become by degrees the owner of all capital, and lease it out to individuals or companies for a fixed percentage, on the security of the undertakings, becoming, in fact, universal debenture-holder, while private persons put all their energies into developing the undertakings, and appropriate all the profit beyond what goes to the State? Of course, at the death of these persons, their interest would again revert to the community; and much of this property that came to the Public would be devoted to public purposes, beneficial equally to all, to town-improvement, to sanitation, education and the like, to everything in a word that would tend to equalise the start in life. So that, ultimately, you would really get what you profess to aim at, liberty for everyone to manage his own life, to take risks, to compete, without any governmental regulation; and that liberty for the first time made really effective for all by the development of equal opportunities.

Stuart. With the trifling objection that, by the abolition of inheritance, you would have deprived men of the principal stimulus which keeps the competitive organisation going.

(e) Unregulated Industry in a Democracy

Martin. Is it the principal stimulus? We have already discussed that. And I maintain that ambition, interest in work, the love of doing well and succeeding, is a far more potent, as well as more honourable motive than the desire to hand on wealth after one's death. Besides, even at the lowest, a man's only chance of acquiring comforts and privileges beyond the average would depend upon his success in conducting his business; and that more, not less, than it does now, since he would not start handicapped by inherited property.

Stuart. But do you really imagine that a man is going to develop a business, and invest a great part of his income in it as capital, when all that he has done will revert to the Public at his death?

Martin. I think that he will do so if you are right in your fundamental assumption that what all men desire more than anything else is independence, initiative and responsibility. They might be offered the alternative, either to become paid servants of the community, taking no risks and contemplating no exceptional rewards; or to engage in business on their own behalf, with the chance of acquiring great wealth, as well as of exercising their abilities at their own discretion subject to no authoritative control. If the former alternative were generally chosen, the society would pass into the type I described, a democratic Collectivism; if the latter, it would be the society based at once upon liberty,

(e) Unregulated Industry in a Democracy

or, as I prefer to call it, automatism, and upon equality of opportunity, which seems to be the logical expression of your ideal.

Stuart. To make a society conform to anything I could consider ideal you must at least allow so much inheritance of wealth that parents may be at liberty to provide for their own children.

Martin. I am supposing that, with the ample funds at the disposal of the community, much that is now done by parents for their children will be done by the Public. But I have no objection to allowing a certain measure of private inheritance, so long as it is kept very small, and does not give differential advantages to the children of the rich. Otherwise, our equality of opportunity is destroyed.

Stuart. And what happens under this system to the equity which you said was to be combined with liberty? For, as I understand, these men who undertake business on their own account may acquire considerable riches.

Martin. They may; but all they acquire will be really the product of their exceptional ability. And exceptional ability, I conceded, in a system based on supply and demand, must get its proportional reward. But, on the other hand, they will not, as they now do, get either rent (save of ability), or interest, or legacies. And, generally speaking, so far as I can see, in this point of equity, the results of the system will be much the same as those produced by my Collectivist State. For if everybody really started with equal oppor-

(e) Unregulated Industry in a Democracy

tunities, educational and financial, so that they could effectively choose their occupation, and if the only superiorities and inferiorities left were those of natural capacity, then though there would be inequalities and distinctions, as there are now, they would be so different from the present ones that the whole face of society would be changed. To begin with, classes would no longer be stereotyped; there would not, in fact, be classes at all, there would only be differences of occupation. And the wages in all occupations would tend to equality. For there would really be that constant flow towards those which for the time being were more advantageous, and away from those which were less so, which Economists postulate as the basis of existent society, but which, as they admit, is rather, so to speak, a pious aspiration than a fact. If, indeed, it be true that first-class ability is very rare, then posts requiring it would still command a high wage; but the general effect would be to raise the reward of the kinds of work that are now badly paid, and to lower that of the kinds that are well paid. And with an equalisation of the standard of life would go an equalisation of manners. Anybody, whatever his occupation, would associate with anybody according to propinquity, or personal attraction, or whatever it might be. The dock-labourer would come home, put on dress-clothes, and sit down to dinner to discuss the latest play or novel with the financier's wife. The professor would go out to the

(e) Unregulated Industry in a Democracy

carpenter's "At Home." The whole society, while it would be mobile and keen in a far higher degree than at present, would be also far more equal and fraternal. It would resemble my Democracy much more than it resembles our present society. And the only important difference between your community and mine would be that the scale of remuneration and of prices would be fixed in the one case by the higgling of the market and in the other by authority.

Stuart. A great advantage on the side of what you are pleased to call my community!

Martin. I do not dispute it; I have no love for authority; I would get rid of it altogether if I could.

Stuart. I understand then, that on reflection you abandon your collectivist Democracy for this other form of society, whatever you may call it?

Martin. Let us call it, if you like, an individualistic, as distinguished from a collectivist Democracy; the names are not good, but that need not trouble us. But as to the point, which of the two I prefer, your society, I admit, has the advantage that it is more completely automatic. The only question is, whether it has corresponding disadvantages.

§ 6. The "Spirit" of the communities that have been considered

Stuart. Of what kind?

Martin. I am not yet sure, but I have a suspicion that if we now proceed to consider what I will call, after Montesquieu, the "Spirit" of the societies we are examining, we shall perhaps find that my community has in this point the advantage over yours.

The "Spirit" of the communities that have been considered

Stuart. I am not clear yet what you are driving at; please explain yourself. For I begin to feel quite a parental interest in this society you have fathered upon me, and am anxious to defend my supposititious child.

Martin. By the spirit of a society I mean so much of its moral attitude as is directly connected with its institutions, so that the one follows from the other.

Stuart. Such a spirit must be very difficult to seize and define.

Martin. Very; but we must try to do it. For it is the flower of the society, that in which its institutions issue and by which they must be judged. So that it must be the last term in my description of the communities we are examining, summing up all that has gone before.

Stuart. Go on then.

(1) The Spirit of Existing Society

Martin. We will start, as usual, with our own society, although it is the most difficult to characterise.

Stuart. Why?

Martin. Because it proceeds from no principle, but from the negation of one. I, at least, after all we have admitted, can only say that all its characteristics follow from its fundamental inequity.

Stuart. How so?

Martin. It is, as we saw, a class-state, which means that everyone is born, without rhyme or reason, into

(1) The Spirit of Existing Society

an advantageous or disadvantageous position. Consequently, the main object of everyone is to rise, as it is called, or to prevent himself from falling. This is true of all the individuals within each class, and also of the classes themselves, in their relations to one another. From this point of view, competition is the most obvious mark of the society; and the inner correlative of competition is egotism. Further, since the fundamental inequity is one of property, the competition is for money; and thus cupidity is its motive—a cupidity intensified almost beyond belief by the fact that the mass of men live on the borders of starvation, while the few, however rich they are, never think they have enough to save them from the possibility of falling to the same level. Egotism, and cupidity—these, then, to begin with, are the most obvious components of the spirit of our society. But again, the class-system involves not only antagonism, but subordination, or rather insubordination. Most people are the employees of other people. And as this relation is not based upon equity, or upon any natural fitness, but upon the accident of birth, the relation between master and servant is one of perpetual discord, veiled or overt. On the one hand is domination, on the other rebellion; insomuch that the only political party which appeals to the great mass of the people and expresses their view of the situation has formulated the character of our society as " class-war." Further, in consequence of these institutions, as we saw, many people live, without working, upon dividends and rents; and this produces, even without our knowing it, an extraordinary moral attitude which I will call, euphemistically, irresponsibility. To receive money becomes to us a kind of sacred right, and how it is obtained a matter of indifference. And this attitude again affects those who are directly conducting business. It is their duty, they hold, to secure dividends, at all costs, for their shareholders. Thus the moral responsibility is tossed backward and forward between the directors and managers, and the receivers of dividends, each rejecting it upon the other. And you get the extraordinary spectacle of kindly fathers, philanthropic spinsters, socialistic dons and professors of moral philosophy, by the accumulated weight of their individual demands for dividends, sweating the lives out of women in hovels and dens of destitution, robbing, torturing, enslaving, murdering whole populations of defenceless natives, and voting indignantly and passionately for the perpetuation of these iniquities under the plea that they are rallying in defence of property. And they are right, for property, in our society, means exploitation; and from that fact follows our whole moral bias. Egotism, cupidity, irresponsibility (which deserves a harder name),—what else shall I add? Isolation! For our class-system cuts us off almost absolutely one from another. Different education, different standards of life, from which pro-

(1) The Spirit of Existing Society

(1) The Spirit of Existing Society

ceed different manners, interests, morals, conventions, partition us into exclusive sections by barriers which philanthropy vainly tries to pass. We meet one another as aliens and strangers; the culture of the artist or professor, the dumb wisdom of the manual worker, each is shut off from the fertilising stream of the other. The intellectual, emotional and spiritual life of every class is impoverished by its isolation from the others; and we creep through life, miserable starvelings, mutilated, marred and ashamed, yearning vainly through walls of glass raised by our institutions for the comradeship that shall quicken and complete our heritage of humanity. Egotism, cupidity, irresponsibility, isolation—shall I go on? It is a long tale and a dreary one.

Stuart. Enliven it then, as you fairly may, by brighter episodes. Speak of co-operation and mutual aid, of kindliness and charity, of public spirit and personal affection.

Martin. Of all these I would be glad to speak in their place; but their place is not here. They do not proceed from our institutions, they are the reaction of human nature against them. They are not components of the spirit of our society, but rudiments of the spirit of the society that shall be.

Stuart. At least you must admit that some good qualities proceed from our institutions—energy, inventiveness, self-reliance, thrift, all that the Economists praise.

(2) The Spirit of an Aristocracy

Martin. I will not dispute it; I do not want to paint my picture over-dark. Let us leave it so, then, with its light and shade, thus indicated in a sketch; and let us turn to the other imaginary societies with which we are comparing it. And first, what about Harington's Aristocracy? If we may disturb him from his reverie to ask him; for I am afraid it is long since our conversation has interested him.

Harington. You do me injustice; I have listened with the closest attention and I am prepared with my answer. I bring forward in defence of the spirit of my society, the most illustrious of names, Plato. Were I an artist as he, I would have made a picture as beautiful as his. But as it is, recall his to your mind, and take it to be mine. For my Aristocracy does not profess to be anything but a transcript from his, or at least, where I have altered the original, the alterations do not affect its spirit.

Martin. Your society, then, like his, proceeds from a principle which you, after him, call Justice; and its spirit, I suppose, we may call that of Order, or better, Harmony, his own favourite term; every class in the community striking its own note, perfectly and infallibly in tune, no other sound possible to it, or by it desired, and all kept exactly strung to the true pitch by the watchful care of the governors—that certainly would be a wonderful instrument for some god to listen to and enjoy! But I am not willing to concede harmony

(2) The Spirit of an Aristocracy

as an exclusive prerogative to your society; for I claim it, too, for mine. There is, however, something else, not found in mine, which is peculiar to yours.

Harington. What?

Martin. Rule and obedience. Everything in your society is ordered by the governing class. They, it is supposed, command perfectly in the interest of the whole; and each part perfectly obeys. There is no tyranny, and no rebellion, but the willing performance of a function recognised as appropriate under a direction recognised as wise and good.

Harington. Yes!

(3) The Spirit of a collectivist Democracy

Martin. And since that attitude proceeds inevitably from your institutions, and they, again, are supported by it, it is the spirit of your society. But the spirit of mine is very different.

Harington. How do you describe it?

Martin. If it were not for Stuart, I should like to call it the spirit of liberty.

Stuart. Oh!

Martin. In comparison, let me at least say, with Harington's. For though, in my society—as also in yours, which in this point I class with mine—the citizens must obey, they obey only their own laws, which they frame and alter as they choose. And these laws are really the same for all, in the sense that all, not some, equally profit by them; and are really made by all, in the sense that no class controls for this purpose the rest of the community. Such a society I call free, in comparison with Harington's; and, so compared, his appears to me like a beautiful statue cunningly moved by the art of the master who created it; while mine presents itself as an organism all of whose parts are alive and make up the life of the whole.

(3) The Spirit of a collectivist Democracy

Harington. I demur to that; I would say rather mine is a true human creature, dominated, as it should be, by the head; while yours is some kind of protozoon whose organs are not yet differentiated.

Martin. Or perhaps mine is superhuman, and every part a man. But I will not bandy metaphors with you. The difference, at any rate, is simple and clear to us all. Every citizen in my society is equally ruler and ruled, and in that sense free; whereas in yours, the governing class rules, and the rest obey. And it is fair to say, if we so understand our terms, that the spirit of your society is authority and of mine liberty.

Harington. Very well.

Martin. But now comes the distinction between Stuart's society and mine; a subordinate distinction, as I think.

(4) The Spirit of an individualistic Democracy

Stuart. Mine, I maintain, is freer than yours.

Martin. I prefer the term used before; yours is more automatic. In mine everyone is an employee of the community, that is to say, each of all. This, I think, is its essential characteristic; and the spirit of its

(4) The Spirit of an individualistic Democracy

citizens, if it achieved its purpose, would be that of the best civil-servant, receiving but not working for a salary; working rather for the work's sake and the public good.

Stuart. Yes, and, as I believe, with all the inertia, obstructiveness and stupidity of civil servants. Whereas my citizens—if I am to adopt them for the moment—would, if such a society could come into existence at all, retain the initiative and energy which is characteristic of our own.

Martin. And retain also its competitive spirit, and something at least of its egotism and cupidity. Something, too, perhaps, of its spirit of tyranny and rebellion, since most men, as now, will be employees of other men; and something of its isolation.

Stuart. Not much, if any, of all this; seeing that, as you describe it, it will be a society based upon equity, and in which no hereditary classes would exist.

Martin. That is true; the evils of this kind will certainly be negligible, compared to what they are among ourselves. Still, competition remaining, and the relation of employer and employed, your society will so far resemble our own, for Good and for Evil. Shall we say then, after this explanation, that the spirit of your Democracy will be self-help, and that of mine public service?

Stuart. I am content.

Martin. It remains then now, having described our societies, to compare them. And first, I would ask, do any of us, does even Stuart, prefer the society we actually have to any of the types we have described? § 7. **A comparison of the communities that have been considered**

Stuart. I should honestly prefer it to Harington's Aristocracy; and I have grave doubts about your Democracy. I will confess, however, that if the society you fathered upon me were to be practicable, I should prefer it to our own.

Martin. I will be content with that. And, on the strength of it, I will suppose our existing society excluded from the discussion; and will go on to the difference between Harington and myself. For I presume that he still prefers his society to mine?

Harington. I confess that I begin to have grave doubts; but I will not give up without a struggle.

Martin. We will try then, Stuart and I, to complete your conversion. For I suppose, in this point, I may count Stuart an ally?

Stuart. Certainly.

Martin. Well, let us proceed to compare these two societies in their principle. We already saw that Harington's Aristocracy was authoritative, and my Democracy, in a certain sense, free. But that did not convince him of the superiority of the latter. And in fact that distinction itself goes back to a deeper one, which we must now bring into relief. What do you

A comparison of the communities that have been considered

say, Harington, is the fundamental principle of your Aristocracy?

Harington. As I have always insisted, and you have agreed, it is Justice, in the Platonic sense. To every member of my community is to be assigned a function exactly suited to his capacity; and that capacity is to be developed by the appropriate education and furnished with the appropriate means.

Martin. I remember that you called that principle justice; and hitherto I have not challenged it. Nor would I do so now, if the question were only one of words. But, in fact, I believe there is something implied in the ordinary use of the word justice which is contradicted by the institutions of your community. And it is important that we should disentangle that.

Harington. What do you mean? What can there be contrary to justice in assigning to everyone exactly the function for which he is fitted, and all the requisite means for performing it? I admit that it is contrary to equality, but that is a very different matter. People now seem to think that every function ought to be accessible to everyone, whatever his capacity. Anybody is to teach, anybody to trade, anybody to govern. But that is not justice, it is injustice.

Martin. Certainly I admit that if really men were fatally produced by nature as narrowly specialised as you suppose your citizens to be; then to organise them as you propose would probably be to come as near justice as would be practicable. But my criticism is that you do not find them so specialised by nature, but deliberately make them so by your institutions. That was the whole object, was it not, of the system of breeding you proposed?

A comparison of the communities that have been considered

Harington. Yes. But what then?

Martin. Why then you, like Plato, having it, let us suppose, in your power to produce men of equal capacities, deliberately choose to produce them unequal; and that is what I think most men would challenge as unjust.

Harington. Surely you can't be unjust to men before they are born? Justice is relevant to actual men. And all I am concerned with is to treat my citizens justly once I have got them.

Martin. But you don't get them on your scheme, you make them. Let me put my point in another way. The first principle of your polity is not really, when we look at your scheme of breeding, what you said it was, the adaptation of function to capacity, but rather that of capacity to function. For you postulate that capacities shall be artificially produced not merely unequal, but elaborately unequal on a narrowly specialised scale. What then is the principle that determines that?

Harington. I suppose what was really influencing me there (though I never before put the question to myself) was the perception that in any society, and especially

A comparison of the communities that have been considered

in a complex one, there must be a number of different functions, and that order demands that to function faculty shall be adapted.

Martin. Really, then your first principle is specialisation, not justice? And that is true also of Plato, whom you follow.

Harington. Perhaps so.

Stuart. Let us look then at this principle of specialisation, and see what we think of it. Do you really judge it to be a good thing in itself that men should be simply tools? That one should pull a lever, another stoke fires, another add up figures, another sweep crossings, and so on through all the occupations of a complicated society, far more numerous and more minute than we can pause to enumerate; each worker being as far as possible fitted to do that one thing and nothing else, fitted indeed so exactly that, as you claim, he will not even feel any desire ever to do anything else, but find his whole demand upon life satisfied by being furnished with the means and opportunity to do precisely that? Is that a picture of men which you like to contemplate, here, as Emerson says, an eye, there a leg, there a stomach, but never a man?

Harington. There is, of course, a certain exaggeration, of which I was myself guilty, in looking at a man simply as a productive agent. Necessarily he is, and in any society must be, also a son and a husband and a father and a friend. He has a life outside his work.

A comparison of the communities that have been considered

Martin. Yes, but that is a life of which the principle of specialisation takes no account, and which it would, so to speak, if it could, put an end to altogether. As, indeed, you will remember Plato, led by the logic of his idea, did actually attempt, forbidding his guardians to be sons or husbands or fathers in any but a nominal sense. But, surely, the truth is that specialisation is not a principle at all, in the sense of an end at which to aim, but at most, up to a point, an unfortunate necessity under certain conditions of production, and one that we should wish, if we could, to confine within the narrowest possible limits.

Harington. I don't think, certainly, that when one isolates individuals or classes and compares them with some ideal Humanity, specialisation seems a good or beautiful thing. But when you look at the whole society, as Plato did and as I was trying to do, then I still think it gives an order which is very beautiful and an end in itself.

Martin. If, indeed, as Plato seemed to think, a society existed in order to be contemplated from without by some æsthetic god! Though, even so, it would, I think, be a very superficial observation which found such a spectacle beautiful. But a society exists for the sake of its members. Its excellence must be judged by their excellence in themselves, and not by some supposed excellence in their relations, which leaves each of them maimed and halt and blind. What is

A comparison of the communities that have been considered

good, surely, is that all men shall be as complete men as possible. And specialisation, so far from being an ideal, is the exact contrary.

Harington. If we could do what we liked I think I should agree with you. But the conditions of life seem to impose specialisation.

Martin. That is no reason, however, why we should exaggerate it as you do.

Harington. What I felt was that, since there must be specialisation, the only way to deal with it, so as to get a good order, is to recognise it frankly and fully and then reconcile it with justice.

Martin. But when it is put to you, do you not agree that the result of that is to form a society of parts of men rather than of men, and that you achieve what you call justice by mutilating humanity? And do you really think that good? Of course, if you do, I have no more to say, except to disagree with you; and we shall have come to an ultimate difference of opinion.

Harington. I cannot honestly say I think it good. But I think that, though bad, it is an element in a scheme of society which is much better at any rate than the actual.

Martin. Perhaps I might not disagree with that. But naturally, like a fond parent, I am anxious to put forward the claims of my own child, and to maintain that it is healthier and more beautiful than yours.

A comparison of the communities that have been considered

Harington. Well, let us go on to yours. What do you say your principle is?

Martin. I will not call it justice, since you have appropriated that word, but I will call it equity.

Harington. Meaning by that?

Martin. Meaning a certain kind of equality between all the members of the society. Only I must make clear what kind. For I do not mean that they should be all alike. There might be innumerable differences of taste and capacity, both original and acquired. But the aim of the institutions would be to secure that these differences should not involve superiorities and inferiorities. There would be relations of friendship as complex and various as you like, but no relations of master and man, ruler and ruled.

Harington. How then are you going to arrange for the necessary subordination involved in any joint enterprise? Will you have no foremen, no managers, no authority of any kind?

Martin. Certainly I must have authority, but not superiority. The man who directs an enterprise will not therefore necessarily stand higher in public estimation, nor will he necessarily receive a greater remuneration, he may even receive less, than some worker in the ranks. He will merely be a man who by natural gifts, or deliberate application, is fitted for that kind of work. Another, perhaps, having equal or greater capacity, did not choose to exercise it in that way, but preferred to do

A comparison of the communities that have been considered

routine work for his living, reserving his higher faculties for some creative work. Thus you might find a man who has chosen for his public and necessary task something disagreeable that others desire to shirk, on condition of being allowed more leisure for pursuing scientific research, or for writing poetry. Such a man would neither despise himself, nor be despised by others, in comparison with the manager of the business in which he was engaged. Both would have the same standard of life, and more or less the same income; both would be educated men of good manners. And the mere fact that the one was under the orders of the other in the part of his life which to him would be least important, would not make him socially inferior, any more than a member of an eleven is socially inferior to the captain. Men would be subordinated in innumerable ways throughout the whole structure of industry; but these subordinations would not constitute class-distinctions, as they do now. For they would not be reflected in a scale of position and power transmissible by heredity and stereotyping, in each new generation, the same distinctions. On the contrary, these industrial subordinations would be recognised for what they really are, mere conveniences; and men would be valued by their broader human qualities as expressed not only in their task-work but in all the relations of life, and especially in those freer and higher activities to which we may reasonably hope, in such a society, far more men than now would be devoted far more intensely.

A comparison of the communities that have been considered

Harington. It is those higher activities about which I feel doubtful. Your equality means an equality of drudgery. You claim, I know, that the drudgery need not, as it does now, occupy the whole time and energy of most men. But I still think it would belittle character. And that brings me back to another aspect of my Aristocracy. In one class there, the governing class, I have ensured that the great qualities of human nature shall be represented. And the basis of these, in my opinion, is the quality of command. By that I do not mean merely what you say you would retain in your society, an authority of convenience over men recognised to be essentially one's equals, but a real superiority felt as such on both sides, involving an impassable distinction of kind, and engendering in the ruler a whole set of moral qualities differentiating him essentially from the ruled. It is this quality and function of command that makes an Aristocracy; and from the dignity and greatness of character thus produced result all the other characteristics I postulate for my governing class, their manners, their taste, their pride of intellect, their noble and self-regarding ethic. "Noblesse oblige," that is the great principle I save for my Aristocracy and you sacrifice to your Democracy.

Martin. This is a new defence you put forward for your society. At first you said its principle was justice,

A comparison of the communities that have been considered

meaning the adjustment of function to faculty. . I then pointed out that really its principle seemed to be the creation of faculty to suit function, and I urged that this implied the deliberate mutilation of men. But now you maintain that one class, at least, is not mutilated, the class of rulers. On the contrary, you say, it represents all the higher qualities of humanity in a way that is impossible under the institutions of Democracy.

Harington. Yes.

Martin. Well, the first point I must raise there is, whether really this activity of ruling is, as you say, the highest. And to do that, we must ask what is the essence of rule, as you conceive it. It is not, if I understand you rightly, the mere act of ordering and directing, which is a necessary function in all society that is at all complicated, and for which I provide in my Democracy as much as you in your Aristocracy. But it is the act of commanding by authority people who obey because they must.

Harington. I postulate that they would obey willingly.

Martin. Perhaps. But they are supposed to have no choice, as well as no desire, save to obey. And it is this fact that makes the difference between direction in my society and authority in yours.

Harington. Well, yes.

Martin. In authority then, or command, or rule, so defined, I do not myself see anything very great and meritorious, though I see a certain greatness in the capacity for organisation and for taking responsibility which I claim will exist also in my Democracy.

A comparison ot the communities that have been considered

Harington. I claim that the habit of command, in my sense of the word, produces a dignity and force of character not otherwise to be developed.

Martin. I cannot see why, unless there were resistance on the part of the governed, and that you rule out. The Aristocracies, or Oligarchies, which I suppose you to have in mind in forming your conception were military, and had the military virtues. It was that that gave them the greatness you postulate, along with much else which you probably do not think desirable. But you, as I understand, are not thinking of a military state. Your rulers would be more like directors of companies. And are they a particularly noble race?

Harington. They would not be like directors, because their motive would not be pecuniary gain.

Martin. Yet the lion's share of the produce of the society, you said, was to fall to them.

Harington. Yes, because they are to be the patterns of the complete life, furnished not merely with necessaries, but with all the materials of magnificence and beauty.

Martin. From that point of view, then, they are to be regarded as art-patrons. For you did not, I think, suggest that they would themselves be artists?

Harington. No, not necessarily. But they would see

A comparison of the communities that have been considered

that an appropriate share of labour and talent was devoted to noble and beautiful things, of which they would be rather trustees for the public than monopolisers for themselves. Whereas, in your society, say what you may, I believe all that side of life would simply drop out, and men would multiply comforts at the expense of art.

Martin. I do not say that is impossible; for I do not know whether the love of beautiful and noble things is a permanent factor or a transitory phase in human nature. And I admit that you have, in your Aristocracy, a class which might succeed in preserving what under democratic institutions might disappear. But, on the other hand, if, as I hope, the instinct for art persists in human nature, then it would have a healthier and nobler development in my society than in yours, just because it would be the spontaneous outcome of popular forces, and not the foster-child of patrons. My Democracy, I believe, would create something like Gothic cathedrals or the town-halls of mediæval Italian cities; while your Aristocracy would create Palladian palaces. However, about all that I do not like to dogmatise, and I grant you the worth of your governing class as art-patrons.

Harington. Then you must go on, I think, to grant me something else, their worth as patrons of pure science and speculation.

Martin. Very well; though that too, I hope, would

flourish also under my Democracy. The argument, I suppose, is the same in both cases. I will even grant you all your case, and admit some extraordinary superiority in the character of your Aristocrats, resulting from the fact that they are rulers. For I want to come back to the point of equity, which seems to me more fundamental. Let us grant that your ruling class does represent the highest type of life; yet others, in your scheme, I suppose represent the lowest; and there is a gradation all the way down, as specialisation becomes narrower and emphasises physical rather than intellectual or moral qualities.

A comparison of the communities that have been considered

Harington. That is my idea, as it was Plato's.

Martin. But now, if you are asked by some Democrat by what right are certain people selected from their birth, or before birth, for honour, and others for dishonour, some to embody exclusively the higher and others the lower aspect of human nature, what will you have to reply?

Harington. I could only reply, as Plato did, that the interest of the whole society demands it.

Martin. But then, if the Democrat replies, as of course he will, "I can construct on my lines a society as harmonious and beautiful as yours, and one free from this defect of inequity"—what will be your rejoinder? Do you admit that this arbitrary distinction between classes, which I am calling inequity, is a defect in your society?

A comparison of the communities that have been considered

Harington. Yes, I think it is a defect, but a necessary one.

Martin. And would it not also be a defect, and one resulting from the other, that between classes in your society, which are to be fixed and hereditary and hierarchic, the emotional relation, though it may be one of harmony, can hardly be one of friendship? For friendship presupposes, does it not, equality, though not identity? It is based on an admiration and a respect which is mutual. And where one is looked up to by the other as superior, both socially and in every other way, the relation, though it may be a good one, will be quite different, like that between master and servant at its best, or patron and client?

Harington. That, I think, would be so.

Martin. Well then, do you or do you not think the relation of friendship the best at which we can aim, however good, in their way, others may be?

Harington. I think perhaps it is the best.

Martin. Does it not follow, then, if all we have said be taken into account, that the democratic ideal is the better one? For I can claim for it that it might secure really as adequate a representation of the higher qualities of mankind as could be secured by your Aristocracy; and even if it did not, yet it would have this great superiority, that it would be founded upon the idea of equity and the passion of friendship which you yourself admit to be good, and which does not seem to be compensated by anything equally good in your Aristocracy.

Harington. I believe, from my admissions, the conclusion would follow, and I accept it for the purposes of this discussion, though I do not know how it may look when I have thought it over again.

A comparison of the communities that have been considered

Martin. Let us leave it so, then; for the comparison of Goods is always difficult, and must be settled by experience rather than by dialectic. But one thing at least, I think, does definitely result from our examination, that the dispute between Democracy and Aristocracy as ideals must be decided, in whatever form it comes up, by the comparative value attached on the one hand to specialisation, on the other to equity; and, with regard to the personal relations resulting in either case, on the one hand to respect or devotion or whatever word may be preferred, and on the other to friendship. These, in the last analysis, are the principles on which the two polities rest, when all secondary considerations have been removed. And it is these, operative in men as passions and ideals, that will, in the long run, decide the issue, and are deciding it now before our eyes.

Stuart. Deciding it which way?

Martin. Deciding it, as I think, in favour of Democracy. That, however, is another point. Meantime, we seem to have arrived at a provisional conclusion to prefer the democratic ideal.

Harington. I assent.

Martin. There remains only the difference between

A comparison of the communities that have been considered

Stuart and myself, which is, I think, much less fundamental, and which I am content to leave undecided. We are both Democrats; and both accept public ownership of land and capital.

Stuart. As an ideal! Of course I don't think it practicable.

Martin. As an ideal, then. But you would prefer that these means of production be let out to private persons to exploit; and I should prefer, on the whole, that the community should exploit them itself. There are difficulties and drawbacks to both solutions, and I am not very tenacious of mine. Still, on the whole, I prefer the attitude of the public servant to that of the private entrepreneur. You are of the contrary opinion. And there I am prepared to leave the matter.

Stuart. I too.

§ 8. The importance of political ideals as guides to practice

Martin. Here then are our types, set up, let us say, like beautiful statues for us to regard and choose between. And now that they are completed, is it not clear, to return to the point from which we started, that it must make a real practical difference which of them it be, or whether it be something different altogether, upon which the eyes of statesmen or of peoples are fixed? For supposing that they were attracted by Harington's ideal, they must go back upon the whole democratic movement, abandon the idea of popular government, and of the equalisation of wealth, and endeavour rather to strengthen classes, and especially the class of the rich, increasing rather than diminishing their wealth and power, and making it more, not less, secure; but endeavouring, at the same time, so to civilise and educate them that they may become worthy to administer it in the public good? To convert what is still in most countries the actual governing class into a true aristocracy would become the aim—a very different one from that which apparently is being pursued in most countries.

The importance of political ideals as guides to practice

Stuart. For that very reason, among others, I have found it difficult to feel much real interest in Harington's society. It seems to me so clearly to have no bearing on actual tendencies.

Harington. I do not agree with you. It is true that, on the surface and in appearance, all parties everywhere accept democratic principles. But that is only because the Oligarchs find that they can best govern in that way. Once they are strong enough, or once their hand is forced, they will throw off the mask and frankly repudiate the whole democratic convention. For at heart all strong men and all rich men mean to rule; they have no belief in equality and in popular government; they hold that a class, or classes of manual labourers on the one hand, and of property owners on the other, is a necessary and desirable feature of every possible society; and so far as they are not mere Oligarchs, and admit no ideal at all, their ideal must be that of Aristocracy.

The importance of political ideals as guides to practice

Martin. That is true, I believe; and in fact already the aristocratic ideal is being aggressively put forward by those ambitious and superior young people who hold themselves to be predestined representatives of the Overman. It is among them, one may suppose, that our Oligarchs, when the time has come, will find their intellectual champions and exponents. Democracy has not won the day, it has hardly begun the battle; for the real fight begins with the attack on property. And in that contest the other party will not be content with the mere assertion of force. They will need a reasoned theory, as did the slave-owners of the South; and, like them, they will find that the only theory which can be at all plausibly maintained is that formulated by Plato of the natural inferiority of certain classes and the natural superiority of others.

Stuart. You don't suggest, surely, that they will adopt all Harington's scheme, with his fantastic system of breeding!

Harington. They would, if they were thorough and sincere. At any rate, this type, which I, after Plato, have set up, is, I am sure, the one to which any theory of Aristocracy must conform that is not merely the cloak of an Oligarchy, and really does aim at a principle of justice.

Stuart. Well, the notion of our millionaires adopting such a theory seems to me a little ridiculous.

Martin. Add to the millionaires the representatives

The importance of political ideals as guides to practice

of the old nobility, the military caste, the aristocrats of intelligence, and all their dependants and clients in the press and church; remember the necessity for every party that is to have moral force,—and moral force in the end is the only force—to represent not merely a fact but an ideal; and perhaps the possibility will not seem so remote. I, at any rate, can quite easily suppose that before long the opponents of Democracy will have the intelligence and the courage to formulate their creed. And if they were able to secure power and direct society as they chose, they would clearly direct it in the way I was suggesting.

Stuart. Well, possibly.

Martin. The other party, on the other hand, for years past have formulated their needs in what is called Socialism. And if they come into power it will be their object to move in the opposite direction, towards what I have called Democracy.

Stuart. That is so.

Martin. But again, among Socialists, it will make a great difference whether they ultimately choose my type of society, or yours. For in the one case they will favour all measures leading to the direct conduct of business by public authorities; and in the other, they will be as much opposed to that as any individualist, while still advocating the public ownership of land and capital. And this distinction, though comparatively unimportant when Collectivism is fighting the present

The importance of political ideals as guides to practice

order, must become, it would seem, one of very great importance within the ranks of the Socialist party.

Stuart. I agree.

Martin. But then, if all this be so, what becomes of your original contention that ideals have no relation to facts? For we seem always to see them determining facts, as the goal must always determine the journey.

Stuart. No; the most I can agree to is that parties formulate ideals. But it is not really the ideals that determine them, nor is it these that get realised. They are, so to speak, excuses or cloaks of more primitive and unreflective passions. Oligarchs may put forward an aristocratic theory, but they don't really mean it; they mean only to acquire or maintain power. So again Ochlocrats (to use your term) may advertise the democratic ideal; but it is not equity that they intend, it is their own advantage. History, as I read it, is a struggle of individuals and classes for power. Ideals are not a cause, they are an effect; they are not an inspiration, they are a pretence. They are sparks struck from the wheel of history. The sparks fly out and vanish, but the wheel turns and turns, hard, material, ruthless, in its substance and motion always the same.

Martin. Here then we have, straight and square, your challenge to me, or rather to history. You say, as I understand, that history has no significance.

Stuart. No ideal significance.

Martin. Well, I do not know what other kind of

significance there can be that could have any interest. However, you deny all force to ideals; and consider it puerile to view either the past or the present as a movement towards their realisation.

The importance of political ideals as guides to practice

Stuart. Yes, I do.

Martin. And you have many and powerful friends to back you. I will not pretend that I can answer you or them in a few words; only the whole of history rightly interpreted can refute or confirm you. But I will do all I can here and now; I will say how the relation of ideal and fact appear to me; and that at least will define the difference between us.

Stuart. Very well, do that.

§ 9. **The relation of ideals to facts**

Martin. First, then, that I may carry you with me as far as possible, I want to admit the full strength of your case. For whatever may be the place and significance of the ideal, it is undeniable that it has to make its way among alien and hostile elements. Let us take, to begin with, the more obvious physical facts. The world is a very small place, and much of it is unproductive. Even where it is productive, it is not always suited for human existence. And even where man can live he can live only by labour, incessant, often degrading, always precarious in its results; for frost and rain, cyclones, floods, tornadoes, eruptions, earthquakes, sweep away in a moment the promise or the fruit of all his toil. The niggardliness and incalculability of Nature, those are the bottom facts; and on that

The relation of ideals to facts

treacherous foundation balances insecurely all our unhappy and hazardous civilisation. It would be different, we should be different, our institutions would be different, if the world were the Garden of Eden instead of the wilderness of Sinai. So that, at bottom, it is Nature, not man, that is responsible for social evil.

Stuart. Yes, that is so.

Martin. That is so; but the rejoinder, you will anticipate, is that the poison has produced the antidote. The brutality of nature evoked the will and the intelligence of man. To every move of hers he had his countermove. He met her forests with the axe, her stubborn soil with the plough, her deserts with the water-course, her sundering oceans with the oar and the sail. From generation to generation the battle has been turning in his favour. He has perfected his armoury, while Nature has neglected hers. The canoe has grown into the ocean-liner; the spade into the steam-plough; the shadoof into the dam of Assouan. If Nature at first was the obstacle, she is an obstacle he has surmounted. If, then, he is still distressed, must not the cause be in himself?

Stuart. No: for with all his running he never comes up with Nature. His numbers, his needs and his desires increase along with his powers; and with all his wealth he is relatively as poor as when first he stood naked on the earth.

Martin. Say so, if you will, though it is not true; and

The relation of ideals to facts

add, if you choose, that the very weapons with which he fights are doled out, with ironical caprice, by the adversary against whom he directs them. No limit, it is true, can be set to the possibilities of science and invention; but those possibilities themselves are at the mercy of Nature. It is she who produces or withholds that conjuncture of the man and the event whence leaps into life the spark we call an idea. Through dark and barren centuries civilisation waited in vain for a Tubal-Cain or a Prometheus, a Gutenburg or a Watt. At this moment there lie, perhaps, in the womb of the future devices which, if they were operative to-day, might realise the dreams of Utopia. But can we by an effort of will hasten or retard their birth? Hazard and chaos are within us no less than without. Our foe is also our creator, and we are the sport of her whims. She will give us a man of genius, as she will give us an earthquake or a famine; but she will do it when and where she chooses. We may wait and starve. No matter! She abides her time!

Stuart. Well, and what can the idealist retort?

Martin. He retorts that, though man cannot control the occasion, he can prepare, or neglect, to meet it when it comes. By his institutions he may make or mar his fate. For they are the channels to carry the sacred fire when it springs, to foster or smother, to husband or to waste it, to lead it to a million exits, lambent and bright and gay, or to choke and obstruct

The relation of ideals to facts

it, or let it idly escape, to waste its heat and light where none can profit. And human institutions, he maintains, all through history, have thwarted rather than aided the conjuncture of genius with chance. From the beginning the mass of men have shared the fate of brutes. They have been slaves and serfs, as now they are wage-labourers. Whatever fire may have slept in their souls, it has found no channel of hope, of opportunity or of ambition, to guide it to the place where it may serve. Not only the caprice of nature, but also the stupidity or iniquity of man has intercepted the currents, the shock of whose meeting is an idea. From before the dawn of history the faculties of the human race have been stunted and thwarted and repressed by the customs and laws under which they have lived. That heavenly visitant, the "chance," has knocked in vain at gates bolted and barred by poverty, servility and fear. Human institutions have sealed the reservoir of the human spirit. Only here and there a jet escaping from an unguarded aperture has hinted at the huge force impotently pent within.

Stuart. Yes, but now comes my point; these institutions too, I say, are not the work of man's will, but the imposition of his fatality.

Martin. His fatality being Nature, who is within him as well as without?

Stuart. Yes.

Martin. Well, let us give full weight to the facts. If

The relation of ideals to facts

man has developed as he has, it is not only because he is placed in such a world as we have described, but also because he is such a creature as we have now to admit him to be. For what do we find him from the first, at the moment he began to take over his own destiny? Was he industrious, peaceful, intelligent, kindly, helpful? No, but a hairy, biped brute, ignorant, cruel, superstitious, split into a thousand tribes and hordes instinctively at feud, so that war and slavery, with all they have carried in their train, were primitive, inevitable, and fatal as the flood and the fire. This was the creature, so framed without his own choice, who laid, as he was bound, the foundations on which civilisation was built. Before he knew what equity was unwittingly he had shaped iniquity; before he could conceive peace, he was plunged in war. From his long sleep in the womb of the brute he opened his infant eyes, to find himself by predestination an enemy, a murderer and a thief. And thus it was, as he grew to reflect, to criticise, and to judge, that he discovered within as much as without the object of his reprobation. He met himself embattled and entrenched against himself. What with one arm he attacked with the other he defended; and the inheritance of the brute, toss and plunge as he may, drags at his heels and hangs about his neck. If now he is split into nations, straining at the leash for war; if now the nations heave and crack in the tension of class conflict; that is because within

The relation of ideals to facts

him work the tiger and the wolf. Because once there were claws and teeth, there are now guns and warships; because once there were capture and rape, there is now prostitution and adultery; because once there were slaves and serfs, there are now wage-labourers. We did not make our institutions; no! Nature made them in us. Even while we criticise them, our brains are silenced by our bellies; and our law of property and inheritance, our manners and morals of sex, are natural facts as obdurate to ideals as the tempest or the volcano. Is something of that kind what you meant when you pulled me up with your protest about institutions?

Stuart. Yes. And now, what have you got to say?

Martin. Only this, which is also true, and the recognition of which—please note it—is what is at the bottom of my difference with you. This animal, Man, this poor thin wisp of sodden straw buffeted on the great ocean of fate, this ignorant, feeble, quarrelsome, greedy, cowardly victim and spawn of the unnatural parent we call Nature, this abortion, this clod, this indecent, unnamable thing, is also, as certainly, the child of a celestial father. Sown into the womb of Nature, he was sown a spiritual seed. And history, on one side the record of man's entanglement in matter, on the other is the epic of his self-deliverance. All the facts, the dreadful facts at which we have timidly hinted, and which no man could fairly face and live, all those facts are true; stop at them, if you will! But true also is the contest of which they are the symbol, real the flood no less than the deposit it has left; real, of all things reallest, the ideal! Do not conceive it as an idea in somebody's head. No; ideas are traces it leaves, shadows, images, words: itself is the light, the fire, the tongue, of which these are creatures. Poetry, philosophy, art, religion, what you will, are but its expressions; they are not It. Thought is a key to unlock its prison, words are a vessel to carry its seed. But It is Reality of Realities, fact of facts, force of forces. It refutes demonstration; it unsettles finality; it defies experience. While all men are crying "impossible," it has sped and done. Even in those who deny it, it lies a latent spark; let them beware the conflagration when the wind of the spirit blows!

The relation of ideals to facts

Stuart. But, forgive the interruption, if that be so, how is it that, in your opinion at any rate, Society, after all these centuries, is still as bad as it is?

Martin. I beg your pardon; I fear I was becoming rhetorical when I wanted, if I could, to be clear. Let me begin again. Looking at the thing as straight as I can, and in what philosophers call a calm moment, I find in men a real fact, the impulse to create the ideal, and this I represent to myself as a seed sown into the soil of Earth with her insufficiency and insecurity, of the flesh with its needs and desires. What therefrom grows up is the tree of human history, receiving its form from the seed, but its matter from the soil and air,

The relation of ideals to facts

warped and stunted, blighted and starved, battered, mutilated, broken, but always straining upward to the light and the sky, and throwing out branches and bearing leaves by the law of its inner impulse. At any moment, then, we may, indeed we must, say, at once that man is a spirit, if we look at his ideal form, and that he is a brute, if we look at his stuff; at once that his Society is bad and that its shaping soul is good; at once that his history is a sordid chronicle of crime, and that it is a solemn school of righteousness. The one is not true and the other false; the truth is the Whole, which I am trying thus schematically to bring before your mind and mine.

Stuart. Well, and then?

Martin. And then, you see, it follows that it is difficult to avoid, if one is sensitive, a constant oscillation between a brutal realism and a blind idealism. For if we observe, day after day, the masses of modern men, walk their mean streets, enter their squalid homes, note them, by myriads, shot at birth into a world so base, peering and peeping in ways of life so narrow and so obscure, and bribed by an impulse of passionate youth to tie the fatal knot that binds them for life to the whirring wheel of drudgery; or if from them we turn to those who seem to be the more fortunate few, and see them too, though they might look up, blind to the sun and the stars, toiling none the less like slaves, or idling like idiots, and ready to shriek with fear and rage if one lift a corner of the veil that shuts out the light from their palace-prisons; if thus regarding this hive of ants, so busy, so mean, so futile, we then turn inward to find in ourselves the swarming fears and needs that explain, though they do not justify, the spectacle; while far above, dim and remote, flickers the flame of the ideal which alone enables us thus to behold and judge; then I confess, in such a mood and under such an obsession, it is impossible not to believe that the ideal is but an idea, and that to attribute power to it is as idle as to suppose that it is the love of perfection that holds the stars constant in their courses. And more and more, in our time, historians and men of letters, and still more those who call themselves men of the world, as indeed they are men of this world, are coming to take and express that view, looking back with a kind of contempt on poets like Goethe or Carlyle, who thought that history was a bible and Nature the garment of God.

The relation of ideals to facts

Stuart. As you too think?

Martin. As I too think, when I am myself. For those who look closer and with a more genial vision find that, in the midst of the evil and squalor, there is also something else, working obscurely and leavening the whole, an impulse of love, however brief, a stress of duty, however circumscribed; that a sap is flowing through wood that seems so dead; and that the faint and flickering lamp of the ideal is lit from fire that

The relation of ideals to facts

burns at the heart of the world. That fire kindles history. Natural facts, economic facts, instincts, needs and desires are the fuel it transmits into a spiritual essence. Always, even in times called of peace, it is gnawing at the roots of society. For it is the never-satisfied; and one of its names is Justice. It is the greatest of all energies; and men of the world call it a dream! It made the French Revolution; it is making revolution now in Russia; it is undermining the whole fabric of western society. One by one it is detaching from the building the buttresses of conviction, and leaving the mere walls of fact that strain and crack to their fall. It is not only, not even chiefly, the working classes that are the strength of that great movement of revolt we call broadly Socialism. Its strength is the weakness of the ruling class, the scepticism of the rich and the powerful, the slow, half-unconscious detachment of all of them who have intelligence and moral force from the interest and the active support of their class. Nay, those who deny Socialism are most under its power; their hollow cries of rage and desperation, their intellectual play with the idea of force, betray their bitter sense of a lost cause. Justice is a power; and if it cannot create it will at least destroy. So that the question for the future is not, shall there be revolution, but shall it be beneficent or disastrous?

Stuart. And so, in the last resort, you end a revolutionist!

The relation of ideals to facts

Martin. I beg your pardon; I must pull myself up, for I have been carried beyond the argument. I was trying to show you how I regard the relation of the Ideal to the Actual, and in what way I think it a real force. I cannot, of course, prove that I am right; but that is what I believe, so far as I can at present formulate it.

Stuart. Yes, I see, more or less, what you are driving at.

Martin. You see, then, also that from this point of view, the Ideal is not utopian, in the sense in which that word is commonly used. It has always reference to contemporary facts, is engendered by and against them, and is itself part of the process that is working out. Though it appear in heaven it is not an unapproachable star; it is the light struck from the friction of contest.

Stuart. Yes.

Martin. And so, in the case of modern Socialism, with which we are concerned, it claims to be not an idle dream but a true prophetic vision, the future with which the present is fatally big; and for that reason it calls itself scientific.

Stuart. Reason small enough, so far as I have been able to discover.

Martin. I do not myself think its science is very correct, nor its necessity very necessary. But so much I think is true, that its hope of the future is based upon the study of the present, and its ideal conceived as the

The relation of ideals to facts

result of a real process. Where it errs, I think, is in the attempt—in a reaction against utopianism—to eliminate altogether the appeal of the Ideal, and to imagine the industrial forces of themselves, independently of human choice, delivering from the womb of the class-war a babe of fraternity and peace. All that, to me, is chimerical. If an ideal is to result, an ideal must be willed; and whether it can result or no is not, so far as we can see, fatally determined, but depends upon our choice. Only that choice must not be made in the void, as of a castle in the air, but here on earth, of a site which we seem to be really able to occupy with materials we really can command. And that, I claim, is the character of the ideal we have been constructing, and that is my justification for regarding it as a guide to action.

Stuart. My doubts, or denials, I have already put forward and I will not repeat myself. What I am interested to learn is how, granted that your ideal is practicable, you will propose to proceed to its realisation. Are you—as I asked a moment ago—are you a revolutionist?

Martin. I am neither good enough nor bad enough for that. I hate discontinuity, confusion, insecurity, as all men do except the best, or worst; and I do not hate the rich as rich, nor the strong as strong, for no men do, except the meanest. I am not a revolutionist; yet I think revolution may come.

Stuart. Certainly it may, if the socialists have their way.

The relation of ideals to facts

Martin. I would say rather, if your friends in the City have their way. At least, if I am at all right in the impression I have received of them, mainly from yourself.

Stuart. What impression?

Martin. Well, it seems to me—I don't know whether I exaggerate—that all the possessing classes, financiers, capitalists, manufacturers, lawyers, professional men, in political issues are singularly uninstructed and unimaginative; that they are as blind to the great equity as they are tenacious of the little, as unintelligent of the whole movement and onward sweep of Society as they are intelligent of those little ripples on its surface, wars and crises, out of which they make their gains and losses. And seeing, in that immense phenomenon called Socialism, which is as much the essence of our age as Liberalism was of the last, nothing but the greed of the poor, the folly of sentimentalists, or the wickedness of adventurers; camping on their possessions, like Fafner on the hoard, in reliance on that enchanted ring, established law and fact; they may indeed, by sheer obstruction, provoke a revolution, in the sense of disturbance, disaster, and ruin for them and for all Society.

Stuart. You admit, then, at least, that a revolution would be disastrous?

Martin. Yes. For I do not believe there is anywhere

The relation of ideals to facts

at this moment any great body of men fit for a better society. To me it is a pure illusion of certain Anarchists, that the wage-earners have either the capacity or the desire to establish to-morrow, by force, an equitable, harmonious and progressive society. Our history and our institutions have produced in us all the same kind of vices and defects. And the working class, I cannot but think, no less than the rest of us, have still, as their main ambition, to make themselves better off than other people; and their idea, like ours, of being better off, is to eat and drink to excess, to dress absurdly and to play stupidly and cruelly. I do not suppose them to be better than the rest of us; they are only at the bottom instead of at the top; and so long as by Socialism they merely mean getting to the top themselves, or at least putting somebody else to the bottom, they are not likely to make a better thing of Society than we have done. There can be no Socialism that has any ideal value till the mass of men in all classes are morally and intellectually converted.

Stuart. That is as good as saying that Socialism is not practicable at all, and means the abandonment of your whole case.

Martin. No! For I believe in conversion, partly conditioning and partly conditioned by a gradual and progressive change of institutions. It is only as against revolution, that is, an immediate catastrophe, that I oppose the facts of human nature as it now seems to be.

The relation of ideals to facts

Stuart. Well, if you come to that, everybody preaches conversion.

Martin. Not in the sense in which I intend it. On the contrary, the pulpit and the press are mostly preaching the opposite; for they are the counsel retained for the present order. I do not mean by conversion that a man should take to going to church, nor even become kindly and charitable, just and honest, within the limits of the current law and morality. I mean a complete change in his whole attitude towards that law and morality, a recognition of it as wrong, or at least as inadequate.

Stuart. Your convert, in fact, will be converted to what the daily press calls theft.

Martin. Certainly he will say with Proudhon "property is theft," not for the sake of epigram or melodrama, but with a deep, clear conviction which will affect all his reactions to every proposal of change. Instead of crying "confiscation" whenever he heard of any project directly or indirectly threatening property, his whole preoccupation would be how to destroy property—meaning of course the present law of property—with the least possible disturbance, confusion, and suffering. If he were a poor man he would consider how the transition could be made easy for those at present in possession; if he were rich, he would consider how it might be made as rapid and effective as possible. Lawyers would plan how to further it,

The relation of ideals to facts

instead of, as now, how to thwart it. Financiers would rack their brains to prevent a crisis, instead of provoking one to terrorise reformers. Manufacturers would work and save harder than ever, not though, but because, their savings were going to the community; and wage-labourers would work with greater responsibility, energy and enthusiasm, as they became the servants of the Public.

Stuart. That would, indeed, be a conversion!

Martin. Yes. For now, we being as we are, what happens and is likely to happen, whenever anything is done or threatened that touches property for the public Good, is an instantaneous rally, unthinking and in the literal sense brutal, of all the propertied classes about any or every abuse out of which they are drawing incomes. Lawyers are at work in a moment to see how the measure proposed may be rendered inoperative; the press is inundated with misrepresentations and appeals to passion; capital is withheld, workmen are thrown out of employment, a social crisis is precipitated, in order that this or that piece of iniquity may continue unchecked, this or that form of robbery and oppression be perpetuated. And all this, remember, is done by good, kindly people, respectable citizens by all our standards, devoted fathers of families, thrifty, prudent, far-sighted men, on whom, as the Economists insist, quite rightly within their assumptions, the maintenance and progress of Society depends.

So perverted are the standards, so inadequate the social code engendered by our institutions.

The relation of ideals to facts

Stuart. It is not, as you have just said yourself, the propertied classes only that are unfit for Socialism. They object to it, no doubt, and in my opinion with justice. But they have, none the less, the kind of qualities which, if they approved it, would enable them to work it. They have public spirit and public honesty, as well as public capacity: whereas the working class has none of these. No sooner do they become employees of a public body than they take the opportunity to malinger and shirk. To do as little as possible for the highest possible wage is all they really have at heart; and whatever be their theory of Socialism, in practice all that it means is exploiting ratepayers in the interest of their own class.

Martin. I shall not attempt to apportion between different classes their due share of social immorality. I do not idealise men who work with their hands, any more than men, like us, who live upon property. That is why I am not a revolutionist; that is why I insist upon moral reformation. Only, as I was saying, the moral reformation I have in view depends upon an intellectual change in our attitude towards our institutions. We have to come to see that they are not final but transitional; not beyond question, but of all things the most questionable. They are our inheritance from the past but they are a bad inheritance, although one

The relation of ideals to facts

that could not have been better. Our business is not to rally round them, but to analyse, dissect and expose them in all their true monstrosity; till, coming to hate them, we come to hate ourselves, who make them possible and necessary, and to determine that we will change in us that human nature which is the whole argument upon which they rest. It is this change in spirit that is the essence of Socialism; as the perpetuation of the present spirit is the essence of the opposition to it.

Stuart. I don't think that is true. Many of us feel a kind of platonic sympathy with Socialism, but we believe it to be impracticable; and that, I think I may fairly say, not because we are prejudiced by class-interest, but on valid objective grounds.

Martin. I am not disputing that many measures advocated by Socialists might, as a matter of fact, if introduced to-day, turn out quite differently from what is anticipated, and result even in disaster. It is no doubt very difficult to forecast, things being as they are, what is likely to be the real effect say of a special tax on land-values, or of a project to create small holders, or of a graduated income tax. Practical statesmen and political economists are bound to consider such proposals with reference to existing facts, and may reasonably and without animus pronounce them impracticable. But this is the point on which I wish to insist; their practicability, or the reverse,

The relation of ideals to facts

depends upon a certain attitude of mind among the people who will have to work them; and that attitude is the basis of all the reasoning. For instance, if those who are affected by a measure regard it as inequitable, they will wish, and very likely may be able, to defeat its purpose, and will do so with a good conscience. Or again, if they treat an arrangement intended for the public Good as an instrument of private advantage, then again they may pervert it from a benefit to a calamity. Impracticability in these cases means that the end proposed by the legislator will not be achieved, even though he passes his law. But this is not the kind of impracticability that might be urged if it were proposed to alter the law of gravitation. It is human nature, not the nature of things, that stands in the way; and human nature is modifiable by human will.

Stuart. Possibly; but if human nature begins modifying its idea of equity, where are we? If there were no other objection to Socialism, there is that fatal one, that it could not possibly be brought into being without intolerable injustice.

Martin. Your objection will serve very well as an illustration of the point I am making. And I reply at once that, in consequence of our institutions, there has grown up among us, I will not say an altogether false, but an imperfect and maimed idea of equity.

Stuart. How do you mean?

The relation of ideals to facts

Martin. I mean that the sense of equity—which is a real and important social force—moves in all classes, but especially among the well-to-do, within the limits of the existing institution of property. The only thing we most of us hold to be really unjust is to take away a man's property without full compensation. It follows that no political cry is so effective as that of confiscation. The mildest project of rectifying, in the most gradual way and with the minimum of disturbance and suffering, some of the inequalities of distribution, at once arouses that cry; so that the notion that socialistic measures are inequitable is, as you say, the first and most fundamental reason why they are impracticable.

Stuart. And a very good reason.

Martin. Good as an obstacle I admit, but not good as a refutation. Not that I wish to deny, as many Socialists do, that confiscation is an inequity; nor will I take the cynical view and point out how seldom that fact has prevented the rich from taking the property of the poor. I will only ask you to recall to your mind all that has resulted from our analysis of property. Property itself, I tried to show and half hoped I had convinced you, is unjust, though we are so used to its injustice that it is hard for us to see it. Nor does it seem that it can ever be effectively transformed without measures which may be truly described as confiscation. So that really there is an ethical antithesis. Are we to perpetuate injustice, or are we to cure it by injustice?

The relation of ideals to facts

And when the question is so put, as I believe it ought to be put, it becomes clear that the fact that a measure is confiscatory is not necessarily a fatal objection to it. The problem is far more complex. We have to ask: " Is the evil involved in the confiscation greater or less than the perpetuation of existing inequity? " The answer to this question can never be simple. But certainly it is not likely that the balance will always be against any confiscation, however mild, gradual and merciful. What stands in our way is the inability or reluctance of men to put the question in that way; and that again depends upon their lack of understanding of the actual evils of Society and their causes; and that again depends upon their obsession by habits and prejudices and interests; and that again upon their lack of imagination, which presupposes and causes a lack of intelligence. So that we come back to what I said; this great obstacle to reform depends upon a mental attitude, and until that is destroyed it is impossible that there shall be any progress.

Stuart. If you destroy that, you destroy the possibility of any society.

Martin. I think not. There can be no society, I admit, without an effective conception of equity. But why must it be just this conception which we have, so poor and inadequate as it is, that the rights of property are for ever inviolable, however immense the wrongs which they involve?

The relation of ideals to facts

Stuart. If they involve wrongs the Community ought to pay the cost of abrogating the wrongs, and so save the rights.

Martin. The Community has not always taken that view, nor always been blamed for not taking it. They gave, for instance, no compensation to the slave-traders. But I do not press that point, for I agree with you that, wherever and up to whatever point compensation can be given without defeating the very purpose of a measure, it ought to be given. But that condition is not present in the case of a transition so large as that contemplated by a revolution in the whole institution of property. For the grant of compensation in full would mean the perpetuation of exactly those rights which I am assuming it to be the object to destroy. If the intention is to substitute public for private ownership of land and capital, it is clearly nonsense to talk of giving full compensation, because that would be to perpetuate with one hand the private ownership which you are destroying with the other.

Stuart. And so, as I said, you fall back upon robbery.

Martin. Why use that language? We are not upon the hustings. We have, if we are Socialists, a definite problem to solve, the creation of an equity at the cost of an inequity. Clearly, the solution must lie in the direction of making the inequity involve as little real hardship as possible. And that could be done, if people were reasonable and patient, by extending the process

The relation of ideals to facts

over a long period of time. The difficulty is that even such a procedure, though the evil it provoked might be negligible compared with the good, would still, in the present state of opinion, be denounced as confiscation and ruled out without further consideration, on the ground of equity, not only by those who would suffer by it, but by many of those who might gain.

Stuart. That is a sign of their sound morals.

Martin. A sign, I admit, that they put morals above interest, and for that they are to be respected; but no sign that their moral conception is the true one. My point is that it is, I will not say false, but inadequate, and that it requires supplementing and correcting by a clear and enlarged view of the inequities of our system of property.

Stuart. Say what you may, what you are really doing is to invite the poor to take the property of the rich.

Martin. It is that way of putting the matter that I think it essential to avoid; for directly it is so put, the Socialist has his reply: "Your present system is the taking of the property of the poor by the rich. I repudiate your equity; I affirm mine; and now, since you will have it, let us fight." And I am bound to say, if it is in that form that the issue is to come up, that the Socialist's position is to me more convincing than his opponent's. But in truth they are both false. Society is not a deliberate exploitation of the poor by the rich; it is a silly, sordid muddle, grown up out of centuries

The relation of ideals to facts

of violence and perpetuated in centuries of stupidity and greed. In many respects the rich are as much to be pitied as the poor, and the poor as much to be reprobated as the rich. If people would come to see that and to feel it, we might really begin to move along. For with the right will we could discover the right means, difficult though that be to do; or rather, with the right will almost any means would become practicable.

Stuart. No doubt, if we were all angels.

Martin. I ask for nothing angelic. I ask that we shall come to understand and judge rightly our society. And if that, which is not at all chimerical, can be brought about by instruction, difficulties of every kind which seem insuperable will soon disappear of themselves. For practically all the objections urged against socialistic measures are based upon the assumption—here and now probably true enough,—that men are stupid and cowardly and greedy and narrow-minded.

Stuart. For example?

Martin. Oh, take any case you like. Say it were proposed, with a view to making the distribution of wealth more equitable, to impose a high progressive income-tax or death-duties. What will happen? Why, we are told, after a certain point capital will emigrate, or men will cease to save, or to work in their old age; production will thus fall off, and more will be lost by that check, even among the very poorest, than could be gained by the more equitable distribution.

Quite possibly that is true. But what does it imply? It implies that men's attitude is such that they will only work and save for themselves and their children but not for the Community. "That is ultimate," you, I suppose, and all your friends would say; and you might even think it satisfactory and desirable. To my mind it is not ultimate, it is rudimentary and barbarous. It is an attitude bred of ignorance and lack of imagination. Let men come to understand, which means to feel as well as to know, what a Society is, how every member is bound up with the whole, how everybody contributes to everything anybody gets, how unprincipled is the present distribution of wealth and opportunity and power; let all this be put to everyone in the language he best understands, not provocatively or with threats, but as a matter of simple fact; and I believe, as the generations go on, the attitude which I deprecate may be modified and transformed.

The relation of ideals to facts

Stuart. It's the old difference between us! You believe in changing human nature.

Martin. I believe that human nature changes in relation to the stages of civilisation; and that nothing is so unscientific and nothing so obstructive to progress as to take the way in which men behave under our present transitional and barbarous conditions, and call it the eternal principles of human nature, conceived to be as fixed and as ultimate as the movement of the earth round the sun. Yet this is what statesmen and

The relation of ideals to facts

even Economists are always doing, in the lightness of their hearts. And that is why they come into conflict with the prophets and the poets. For these latter are the rebels who assert against Man as he is, Man as he shall be and must be. They are the sap pressing up in the tree of Humanity; they are the growing points feeling out into the light. "This tree is dead wood," cries the practical man, and the man of science echoes him. "No, no," says the poet, "this tree lives. Something in it is pushing outwards; there lie in it buds and leaves; what it is it shall not be when the spring comes. I know, I know, I know, though I cannot prove."

Stuart. That may be all very well for a poet; but it is not the attitude or language of a statesman.

Martin. Not of our statesmen of to-day, but perhaps of our statesmen of to-morrow. For what we are all suffering from, more than from anything else, is the divorce of poetry from life and of imagination from practice.

Stuart. Perhaps; but the remedy can hardly be to act poetry and imagine facts.

Martin. No; but to transform our inner life by the power of imagination, as we are transforming the outer world by the force of science. Except in so far as that is done there can be no real progress; and when it is done, and in proportion as it is done, how different will become the tone of electors and of politicians and of the

The relation of ideals to facts

press on all the subjects we have been discussing! I am going home to-morrow to vote, with little enough enthusiasm, for I know, men being as they are, how little anyone can do. But I hear in my heart all the time such a speech as has never been delivered, and feel a response such as has never yet been evoked.

Stuart. Let us have the speech.

Martin. Will you promise me the response?

Stuart. I make no promises. Give me the speech.

Martin. I cannot catch that eloquence from those far heights. But I will tell you the substance of what I seem to hear. Imagine the great man, imagine an electorate instructed at last by years of barren strife, imagine the auspicious moment, imagine the voice of passion. "Fellow citizens," thus the orator begins—"I stand before you to demand a mandate for revolution. The time for petty measures, for insincere talk, for burking principles and disguising purposes, is past. I am here to announce my desire and my intention, if you will give me the commission, to inaugurate a scheme for altering the whole basis of property. The reasons that have driven me to this position are familiar to you, and weigh, I believe, as strongly with you as with myself. The conditions under which we are living are admittedly preposterous. A few of us have far too much, some of us enough, but most of us far too little. Those who have very little work hard for it, when they are allowed, all day and every day, at the most disagree-

The relation of ideals to facts

able, dangerous and exhausting labour; or else, not being even allowed to work, people our workhouses and prisons, or join the criminal class, or starve. Those who have too much, work too, some of them, very hard, but at the more pleasant and stimulating kinds of labour; others do not work at all, but devote their lives to ruining themselves and their dependants. This distribution of property and labour, further, is in effect hereditary; for the children of the rich are brought up with every advantage of education and opportunity, and those of the poor with every disadvantage. Our society is thus a handicap, but one based on no principle; for it is the birth, not the capacity of the runner, that determines his start. This state of things used to be described as one of free competition; but we have learnt to call it by its true name, social anarchy. We all deplore it; we all wish to alter it; but, to tell the truth, we are afraid to do so. For we see that to do it we must attack property; and although our law of property is the source of all our inequities, yet we see it to be the foundation of our society, and we fear that if we tamper with it the whole building will come down about our ears. This fear we must put away from us. It will be my business, if I win your confidence, to plan, with the advice and assistance of our ablest practical men, such a scheme of transition, as will lead us, without serious disturbance or shock, over to a better and more equitable social condition. I do not doubt that this can be done, if we seriously will to do it. But we must will it all of us, both those who stand immediately to lose and those who stand to gain. It is no party scheme which I invite you to commission me to draft; it is no plan for plundering the rich by the poor. No! It is a plan to prepare the way for a more prosperous, a more free, a more noble community, by the willing co-operation of all classes.

The relation of ideals to facts

"I invite you all, and, first, I invite the rich. Now is their great opportunity. I appeal, and I appeal with confidence, to their chivalry; I go further; I appeal to their true interest. Are they happy as rich men? Is their conscience at ease? Is their life large, adventurous and noble? Do they meet friends wherever they go? Are they loved and respected? Or are they not rather camped among enemies, isolated, envied or despised, cut off from communion with their kind, from the great human passions and the great human needs? Is it with satisfaction that they see their children entering upon life, spoilt from the cradle, untrained, undisciplined, unrefined, unfit for work, incapable of pleasure, selfish, narrow, frivolous and false? To them and to their children I offer the great chance, I offer them the interest of active co-operation for the public good. To their souls, seared and seamed by drought, I offer the water of life. I offer them the opportunity to be patriots. Is it not an opportunity

The relation of ideals to facts

worth paying for, and paying high? Yet I offer it cheap. No sudden loss shall fall upon them. Their children, it is true, and their grandchildren unborn will start from the ranks; the happier they! But the rich men now among us will continue to be rich, and their children now grown-up will not be poor. We shall proceed gradually and with discretion in the redistribution of wealth; and what we ask from the rich is less an immediate money-sacrifice than the active co-operation of the ablest among them in discovering the most statesmanlike method, and the loyal acquiescence of them all in the scheme that is finally adopted.

"To the poor I have a different message. I have to ask them, first, as they have waited patiently for generations, to wait yet another half century; to be content to view the promised land into which not they, but their children and their children's children will enter. They have the power of numbers; but that is not enough; they need the power of ability. Without the willing co-operation of the captains of labour nothing effective can be done; on grounds of policy, as well as on grounds of equity, we cannot afford to alienate them by measures which they regard as confiscation. That appeal then I make to you, the appeal for patience and fairness. But it is the least of what I have to ask. I call upon you to rise to the height of the new opportunities opening before you. Hitherto you have worked under the lash of fear for yourselves

The relation of ideals to facts

and your children; henceforth learn to work under the stimulus of citizenship for the public Good. Take full advantage of the chances now beginning to be offered in a cheaper, a better, a more practical education to learn well not merely your trades, but your place as members in the body of Society. Acquire responsibility, and with it dignity. Let shirking, cheating, corruption become among you offences against your own self-respect, no less than against the Community. Let the law, made henceforth by and for yourselves, become to you as your own will. The future for which I invite you to prepare is not one of mere prosperity; it is not even one of mere equity. It is a future of conscious and proud public service. What we offer is the charter of your spiritual liberty; make yourselves and your children worthy of it. We open the gates of the temple of Humanity; make yourselves clean that you may enter in.

"And this I say, in conclusion, to all of you, rich or poor. Henceforth, in principle, classes are abolished. No kind of work is base, though many kinds must be onerous; and because his work is onerous no man, in the time that is coming, shall be, as he is now, poor and despised. To make work honoured and leisure noble, henceforth is the business of us all. It is also our inspiration and our joy. The age of languid effort, of indifference, monotony or despair, of opiate pleasures and base excitements, is passed. Life remains incom-

The relation of ideals to facts

prehensible, but it becomes great. The purpose and sense of it is at our doors, clangorous and clear as a trumpet. To work as we shall work, to use our leisure as we shall use it, carries with it its own justification. Outside is the mystery; but within us the call, and by our institutions the means to fulfil it. What more need we ask in the span of our brief lives? The challenge I fling to you is the greatest to which ever men have been invited to respond. It is the challenge to put off your gait of the mill-horse pacing his round; it is the challenge to live of your own motion, like free spirits as you are; it is the challenge to use institutions, instead of being used by them; it is the challenge to unseat things from the saddle of destiny and to seat there instead the human soul. Is it not worth sacrifices, if sacrifices be involved? Is it not worth effort, thought, imagination, faith? What in comparison are our petty quarrels about yours and mine? You and I alike own nothing but ourselves. Of that let us make ourselves masters; the rest will be added unto us!"

Stuart. Is that all?

Martin. All I can reproduce, here and now.

Stuart. Well, I only ask you not to try it on the platform when you get home.

Martin. I do not speak like that on the platform; but I never speak without that, or something like it, singing in my heart. It is the same tune that the stream sings to me, day by day, that the pine-trees whisper and the mountains echo.

The relation of ideals to facts

Stuart. Preposterous man! And have the stream, the pine-trees and the mountains been singing to you which way to vote?

Martin. O yes! That is why I am going home.

Stuart. And may one ask what their counsel was?

Martin. You may ask. But I am protected by the ballot.

THE END